A DEBATE

Between

W. L. OLIPHANT

Minister, Oak Cliff Church of Christ, Dallas, Texas

and

CHARLES SMITH

*President, American Association for the Advancement of Atheism,
New York City.*

Held in the Church of Christ, Shawnee, Oklahoma.

1929

Cobb Publishing
Charleston, AR
www.CobbPublishing.com
CobbPublishing@gmail.com
479-747-8372

ISBN: 979-8-3303-2352-4

Propositions

1. **"There is a Supreme Being (God, Creator)."**

- *Affirmative:* W. L. OLIPHANT.
- *Negative:* CHARLES SMITH.

2. **"Atheism is Beneficial to the Race, and is most conductive to Morality of any Theory Known to Man."**

- *Affirmative:* CHARLES SMITH.
- *Negative:* W. L. OLIPHANT.

3. **"All Things Exist as the Result of Evolution, Directed by no Intelligence."**

- *Affirmative:* CHARLES SMITH.
- *Negative:* W. L. OLIPHANT.

Chairman: F. L. PAISLEY.

Table of Contents

Publisher's Preface

Not everyone is so situated that they can know what is going on through the length and breadth of our land. Few are in positions where they can feel the pulse of public sentiment and observe conditions that are conspicuous in social and religious circles. As the publisher of a journal of wide circulation I have been fortunate in being able to observe conditions, including dangers that face our great country whose foundation has been the fundamental truths of God's Holy Word. When men with dangerous imaginations began to destroy the faith of weak ones the older ones naturally sensed the alarm and have been on the defensive. The dangers have become so great that they must be met and handled as open foes. I have seen from every direction an alarming tendency on the part of the careless, unthinking, pleasure-bound people to take up with the theories of modern Atheists and because of their liberal and loose views on many moral subjects give up their love for and joy in Christian doctrine and practice. The great mass of people are giving little thought to religious matters, and the advent of atheistic teachings has contributed its large part in breaking down the faith of those who were easily influenced and didn't have the depth of thought to know and enjoy the strength of the Christian doctrine. The present generation are not rooted and grounded in God's eternal truth, therefore it is easy for ideas that recognize no day of accounting to give in and give way and follow the line of least resistance in the enjoyment of everything that satisfies for a time those who have no fear of God or eternity.

We who are older and have seen real life and have seen cowards and brave men die, know that in the last day there will be gnashing of teeth and terrible distress of mind when such deluded creatures will cry out in their agony and dismay—"Lord, have mercy!" Such would not believe the Savior if one came from the dead, but in that last day and before this mortal flesh is laid in the ground, every last one of them will call to God for mercy and salvation, but there will be none.

The circulation of a book like this debate must do a world of good, and we send it forth with the' only thought and purpose that it may open the eyes of those who are in darkness and who have been so easily led away from the teaching of Godly parents.

F. L. ROWE.

Introduction

"The Oliphant-Smith Debate"

On August 15 and 16, 1929, there was held at Shawnee, Oklahoma, a debate between W. L. Oliphant of Dallas, Texas, and Charles Smith, President of the American Association for the Advancement of Atheism. Three propositions were discussed during the debate. Proposition 1: "There is a Supreme Being (God, Creator)." Affirmative: W. L. Oliphant; Negative: Charles Smith. Proposition 2: "Atheism is Beneficial to the Race, and is the Most Conducive to Morality of Any Theory Known to Man." Affirmative: Charles Smith; Negative: W. L. Oliphant. Proposition 3: "All Things Exist as the Result of Evolution, Directed by No Intelligence." Affirmative: Charles Smith; Negative: W. L. Oliphant. I have read the manuscripts of all the speeches made during this debate. I enjoyed heartily the reading of the manuscripts, and I am pleased to have the privilege of writing a short introduction to the book.

W. L. Oliphant is a member of the Church of Christ, and is located with the Oak Cliff congregation in Dallas, Texas. He is a young man—

physically strong, mentally bright, and well educated for the work of a preacher. He is deeply spiritual, and believes with all his heart in the absolute truth of the Bible. His speeches bear unmistakable evidence of his faith, as once for all delivered unto the saints. His manner in debate, as everywhere else, is courteous; for he is a polished gentleman, as well as a scholar.

Charles Smith, by virtue of the position which he holds, should be a fair representative of the atheistic view of life. Considering his views, I think that he behaved with commendable courtesy during the discussion. It is a pleasure to state that at no time daring the discussion did the debaters descend to discourteous treatment of one another. Brother Oliphant acquitted himself with high credit, both as to the manner and matter of his speeches. He took the debate seriously, and in his opening speech pitched it upon a high plane. It was evidently his aim to make the discussion one that would be worthy of the attention of all thoughtful people. I am sure that in his part of the debate he succeeded nobly.

The speeches made by Charles Smith in the discussion of the first two propositions do not seem to me to have done justice to the side which he represents. I have no sympathy for his position on any of the propositions; but I do like to feel that even an opponent does credit, or at least justice, to the side for which he contends. Mr. Smith's speeches on propositions 1 and 2 consist, in the main, of finding fault with certain doctrines and practices of professed Christians of all religious bodies, or of bringing forward accusations against the truthfulness and purity of statements found in the Bible. I do not know why he pursued the course which he did; but he excited sympathy in my mind for himself by the very weakness of his efforts, as revealed in his speeches on the first two propositions. It is easy enough to find faults with all professed Christians, and it is just as easy to misinterpret Bible statements and make them say things which any fair minded person would condemn. Perhaps Mr. Smith did the best he could. If this be true, the cause which he represents should see to it that he prepares himself to represent the cause for which he pleads in a more creditable manner so far as his arguments are concerned.

In discussing the third proposition, in which Mr. Smith was affirmative, the truth of evolution, he did his best work. It seemed to me that this was the only proposition upon which he had material appropriate to the discussion; but even in his speeches on evolution, his arguments in the main were old and many of them have been discredited for a long time, so that they are no longer used by up-to-date proponents of evolution.

It was a pleasure to see how skillfully Brother Oliphant followed Mr. Smith through every one of his speeches, and answered with force and clearness every argument and even every quibble of his opponent. I am sure that those who believe the Bible to be true and who have faith in God, will be pleased with the manner in which the representative of their side conducted himself personally, and also with the masterly manner in which he handled his part of the argument. He showed himself at all times to be well acquainted not only with his own side in the discussion, but also with the side of his opponent.

The book embodying this debate is being printed by the Christian Leader Publishing Co., 422 Elm St., Cincinnati, Ohio, with Brother F. L. Rowe as publisher. I trust the book may have a large sale. It will be especially interesting to preachers and to mature church members and officers. Books of this nature are net intended for children or immature minds. It is a question how far the publishing of atheistic views, even when presented in well conducted discussions, is profitable. There *are* those who think that the very publication of such views gives them a circulation wider than they would perhaps get in any other way. There are certain people upon whose minds a familiar or irreverent handling of sacred things works a feeling of contempt. But it is the boast of Christianity that its views do not shun the light of the most searching investigation, whether coming from friends or foes.

It is not likely that very many children or immature persons would enjoy a discussion of these themes; hence the book is not likely to work any injury upon such minds through the danger just alluded to. People with sufficient intelligence to appreciate the argument presented in this debate will be strengthened and greatly encouraged by the splendid showing made by Brother Oliphant against this champion of atheism. I trust that many of our preachers and teachers and thoughtful church members will buy the book and read it. Praying God's blessing upon all who may read it, I am with brotherly love,

HALL L. CALHOUN,

Belmont Blvd. and Observatory Drive,

Nashville, Tennessee.

October 8, 1929.

Explanatory Statement

In offering to the public a discussion of the existence of God, I feel much as did Alexander Campbell about his debate with Robert Owen. In his first speech, Brother Campbell explained that he did not intend by engaging in such a discussion to seem to admit that the Christian religion is in need of defense, or that there are reasonable grounds for the rejection of Christianity. God's Word has nothing to lose by its being contrasted with the theories of its enemies. Truth is never so beautiful as when seen in contrast with falsehood. In this debate I have tried simply to present truth, and allow intelligent people to decide between it and what Mr. Smith offered.

I do not pretend to have exhausted the subjects discussed. In fact, the evidence on the Christian side of this question is so abundant that I was not able to offer more than a small percentage of the material available. I believe, however, that the honest student will find in my speeches enough evidence of the existence of God and the truth of the Bible to thoroughly ground him in the faith. While I cannot comprehend God, I can acquire working knowledge of His will, which is sufficient for the battles of life. It is said that Rowland Hill was once trying to convey to his audience the greatness of God's love. Suddenly he stopped and raising his eyes heavenward, exclaimed: "I am unable to reach this lofty theme. Yet I do not think that the smallest fish in the ocean ever complains of the ocean's vastness. So it is with me. With my puny powers I can plunge with delight into a subject the immensity of which I shall never be able to comprehend."

Mr. Smith has been very fair about the publication of the debate. He went so far as to say in a letter: "If there is any atheist argument which I have failed to present that you especially desire to refute, put it in my speech where it will fit, and then reply to it in yours." However, I have not taken advantage of this offer. His speeches appear just as corrected by him. By mutual agreement some material has been added to the speeches on the last proposition. I speak much faster than Mr. Smith speaks. This explains the fact that my speeches occupy more space in print than his.

If it seems that I have given undue notice to the degrees and other evidences of scholarship of the men I have quoted, I explain that I did this bemuse of Mr. Smith's charge that educated people do not believe in God. I am glad to have the introduction written by Hall L. Calhoun. Brother Calhoun is a scholar. He is a graduate from the College of the Bible at Lexington, Kentucky; a graduate from Yale Divinity School, at New Haven, Connecticut, and has an M. A. and a Ph. D. from Harvard University.

I am much indebted to the good brethren at 3hawnee, Oklahoma, for their co-operation. Brothers Will J. Cullum and F. L. Paisley contributed much to the success of the debate. I appreciate the splendid stenographic work done by Miss Blanche Burton in reporting the speeches. I am also grateful to Mr. and Mrs. M. L. Petty and Mrs. E. L. Fisher for their assistance in the preparation of the manuscripts. For the material used in the speeches I am obligated to many authors. Many direct quotations from others were used. In these cases, I have given credit to the authors by citing names of books and pages on which quotations are found.

I send this volume forth, asking only a fair examination of the arguments presented; and praying that it may be instrumental in leading some skeptic to faith in the living God, and in strengthening and encouraging Christians. Rest assured that God's Book will stand any test applied to it. The feeble blows of infidelity, such as those made by Mr. Smith, will not so much as leave a scar on the Book of God or the Church of God.

"Last eve I passed beside a blacksmith's door
And heard the anvil ring the vesper chime;
When looking in, I saw upon the floor,
Old hammers worn with beating years of time.

" 'How many anvils have you had,' said I,
`To wear and batter all these hammers so?'
`Just one,' said he; then said with twinkling eye,
`The anvil wears the hammers out, you know.'

"And so, I thought the anvil of God's word
For ages skeptic blows have beat upon;
Yet, though the noise of falling blows was heard,
The anvil unharmed—the hammers gone!"

Sincerely,

W. L: OLIPHANT.

God vs. Atheism

(Thursday evening, August 15, 1929)

Proposition:

"There is a Supreme Being (God, Creator)."

Affirmative: W. L. Oliphant
Negative: Charles Smith.

Preliminary Statement

The meeting was opened by Brother Will J. Cullum, minister for the Shawnee Church of Christ. After a brief introductory speech, he introduced Brother F. L. Young, minister for Tenth and Francis Streets Church of Christ, Oklahoma City. Brother Young lead the congregation in prayer.

Brother Cullum then introduced Brother F. L. Paisley, minister for the Church of Christ, Seminole, Oklahoma. Brother Paisley served as chairman throughout the debate.

After a few words in explanation of the propositions for debate, the order in which the speeches were to be delivered, etc., Brother Paisley introduced Brother W. L. Oliphant, the first affirmative speaker.

Oliphant's first Affirmative

Mr. Chairman, Ladies and Gentlemen, Respected Opponent:

It is now my happy privilege to stand before you in defense of a proposition which I believe as firmly as I believe any proposition I have ever considered. I am here to affirm the existence of God, the Creator of the universe, the omnipotent Personality, "in whom we live, move and have our being." I realize that with a vast majority of you, as is true of any intelligent audience in this country, there is no need of my offering proof of this proposition. Your minds are fully convinced of its truthfulness; you believe for reasons—the sufficiency of which you have never had occasion to question—not only in the existence of God, but in His power and goodness.

I am glad to see such a large audience. I regret that because of lack of room, some have been turned away. I am especially glad to see in the audience many of my friends from various sections of the State. I appreciate your presence, and thank you for the interest that prompted your coming to hear this discussion. Let me say in the very beginning of the debate, that for Mr. Charles Smith, my opponent, I hold nothing but the most kindly feeling; for his degrading doctrine of atheism, I have the utmost contempt.

The terms of the proposition I am to affirm are so simple that I presume no defining or explaining is necessary. However, that the precise point at issue may not escape the attention of any one, I shall say a few words along that line. I am under no obligation to comprehend and explain God. I cannot do so. In fact, if finite mind could comprehend Him, He would not be an infinite God. The infinite cannot be completely grasped by the finite. So far as the proposition is concerned, I need not discuss the methods of God's operations. I am under no further obligation than to prove the existence of Him Who is the Creator.

I should like to emphasize the fact that I am not under obligation to defend degradations or counterfeits of the religion of Jesus Christ, any more than a government is obligated to defend counterfeit coins. Really, the Christian religion should not be brought into the discussion of the present proposition, except perhaps, incidentally; but I feel that it is good to warn my opponent at the very outset that I shall not at any time attempt to defend sectarianism, even though it poses as the religion of the Christ. I have no sympathy or love for de-nominationalism.

THE PRINCIPLE OF FAITH

It should be understood that my proposition must be accepted as a matter of faith. We cannot demonstrate God to the senses. He must be accepted by faith. The writer of Hebrews says faith is "the evidence of things not seen" (11:1); and in Romans we are told that "faith comes by hearing" (10:17). My duty then, is to examine the evidence upon which we accept the existence of God; and to determine whether our belief in God stands upon a reasonable basis. We are not the only ones who act upon the principle of faith; even the atheist does that Anything that is not susceptible to demonstration to any of the five senses can be accepted only by an act of faith; even the atheist must accept many things upon the principle of faith.

Consider electricity. George D. Shepardson, A.M., M.E., Sc.D., late Professor of Electrical Engineering, University of Minnesota, *says:*

> "The mind of an electrical engineer at once reverts to the fact that we cannot see electricity, nor do we hear, taste, smell or feel it directly, yet we have a great deal of knowledge about it.

—Electricity has long since become a relatively exact science and art, notwithstanding the fact that electricity is not directly manifest to a single one of our commonly recognized senses." (The Religion of an Electrical Engineer, pg. 38.)

So, while we light our homes and streets with electricity, and use it in various and sundry ways, still we must accept some things about it as matters of faith.

Some of the very finest principles of life must be accepted largely by faith. Who ever saw "hope"? No one; and yet, hope of some kind is enjoyed by every sane human being. We have never seen the principle of "patriotism." "Love" is not perceptible to any of the five senses. Who doubts the existence of "mother love"? Still, you have never seen that principle. You have witnessed some of its workings, but the principle itself escapes actual contact with any of the physical senses.

All persons and incidents of the generations past are accepted by us on the principle of faith. We hear the evidence concerning them, and then formulate our belief or faith regarding them. I accept the facts that Napoleon Bonaparte lived and ruled and that George Washington was first president of the United States, but I never saw either of those gentlemen, nor have I seen anyone who did see them. I have evidence of their having lived; and I accept the facts of their lives because of this evidence. Only by faith do I know of these men. He who denies faith must refuse to accept *as* facts everything which he himself has not observed. All historical information must be set at naught.

ABSURDITY OF ATHEISM

The absurdity of the atheist's position is evident on its face. We might exercise some patience with the man who is honestly an agnostic, the *man* who says, "I do not know"; but the man who boldly claims to KNOW that God does not exist, takes an absurd and ridiculous position. If there is one thing he does not know, that thing may be that God exists. If there is one place in all the universe he has never been, God may be in that place. Before a man can consistently deny the existence of God, he must make a god of himself. He must declare that he is infinite in knowledge—that he knows everything. No man can consistently say these things. Therefore, no man can consistently declare that God is not. The doctrine of atheism is preposterous and absurd.

HISTORICAL EVIDENCE

Man is incurably religious. No nation or tribe of people has been discovered that does not believe in some kind of Supreme Being, and practice some form of religion. We may go farther, and say that in all the religions of earth there are traces of monotheism—belief in one God. No matter how polytheistic we find a people, nor how deeply enshrouded in darkness their religion is, there are always faint, glimmering rays of a purer light. In the midst of the belief in many gods we find relics of the faith of a previous time—a pure monotheism. It is also worthy of note that the earlier forms of the various heathen religions are purer than the later forms. Principal Fairbairn, of Oxford, lays down this general rule with regard to historical religions:

> "The younger the polytheism, the fewer its gods." (Studies in Philosophy of Religion, pg. 22.)

Dr. James Orr, Professor of Apologetics and Systematic Theology, United Free Church College, Glasgow, quotes this rule, with approval, and says:

> "Man's earliest ideas of God were not, as is commonly assumed, his poorest.—No savage tribes are found who do not seem to have higher ideas of God along with their superstitions. Man does not creep up from fetishism, through polytheism, to monotheism, but polytheism represents rather the refraction of an original undifferentiated sense, or consciousness, or perception, of the divine.—In the oldest religions, without exception, along with the polytheism, we find a monotheistic background." (The Problem of the Old Testament, pg. 496.)

Hear Dr. W. M. F. Petrie, D.C.L., LL.D., Lit.D., Ph.D., F.R.S., F.B.A., F.S.A., Professor of Egypt- ology, University College, London:

> "Were the conception of a god only an evolution from such spirit worship (referred to on previous page) we should find the worship of many gods preceding the worship of one god,

polytheism would precede monotheism in each tribe or *race*. What we actually find is the contrary of this, monotheism is the first stage traceable in theology. Wherever we can trace back polytheism to its earliest stages we find that it results from combinations of monotheism." (The Religion of Ancient Egypt, pg. 4.)

I next offer the testimony of Dr. E. W. Hopkins, Ph.D., LL.D., Professor of Sanskrit and Comparative Philology, Yale University. He says:

"That religions may all be traced back to one primordial religion is not wholly a narrow 'orthodox' view. In this form, however, it is still held by both the Hindu and the Christian of very conservative type. For example, about two thousand years ago Manu, the Hindu law-giver, declared, what is still believed by orthodox Brahmans, that one true religion was revealed to man in the beginning and that all later types of religion have *been* vain divergences from this divine model." (The History of Religions, pg. 14.)

This author then quotes from "Fetishism in West Africa," by Dr. R. H. Nassau, pg. 23. Here is the quotation:

"All religions had but one source and that a pure one. From it have grown perversions varying in their proportions of truth and error."

We shall next listen to Dr. William A. P. Martin, of the Peking University. Dr. Martin discusses the evolutionary theory of the origin and development of religion, and then adds this significant statement:

"This theory has the merit of verisimilitude. It *indicates* what might be the process if man were left to make his own religion; but it has the misfortune to be at variance with the facts. A wide survey of the history of civilized nations (and the history of others is beyond reach) shows that the actual process undergone by the human mind in its religious development is precisely opposite to that which this theory supposes; in a word, that man was not left to construct his own creed, but that his blundering logic has always been active in its attempts to corrupt and obscure a divine original." (The Chinese, pg. 163, 164.)

This author continues at length in his discussion of the question. He shows that the religious rites of the various countries bear "unmistakable resemblance, suggestive of a common source."

Professor Max Muller, famous Oxford professor, discusses in a similar way the lapse of mankind from earlier and simpler types of belief to low and manifold superstitions. He says:

> "Whenever we can trace back a religion to its first beginning we find it free from many of the blemishes that offend us in its later phases." (Chips from a German Workshop, Vol. 1, pg. 23.)

We might continue almost indefinitely such quotations regarding religions, generally. An examination of the religions of specific nations further confirms our position that all religions are degenerate forms of an original pure monotheism. Let us look at the religions of some of the nations.

Egypt

Dr. Budge, keeper of the Egyptian and Assyrian antiquities in the British Museum, tells us that as late as the Fourth Dynasty the number of gods worshipped in all Egypt was about two hundred. In the Nineteenth Dynasty, Thebes alone had about twelve hundred, and there were hundreds of other local gods in other religious centers. He adds:

> "The sublimer portions are demonstrably ancient; and the last state of the Egyptian religion, that which was known to the Greek or Latin writers, heathen or Christian, was by far the grossest and most corrupt." (Renouf, "Hibbard Lectures,' pg. 91. Quoted by Dr. John L. Campbell, in "The Bible Under Fire," pg. 89.)

An Egyptian inscription which supposedly belongs to a period fifteen hundred years before Moses says regarding God:

> "He has made all that is; thou alone art, the millions owe their

being to thee; he is Lord of all that which is, and of that which is not." (Quoted by Dr. F. F. Ellinwood, "Oriental Religions and Christianity," pg. 250.)

India

The Rig-Veda contains the most ancient hymns of India. In the 129th hymn of the tenth book there is a very clear expression of monotheism. It reads:

> "In the beginning there was neither naught nor aught Then there was neither atmosphere or sky above, There was neither death or immortality,
>
> There was neither day nor night, nor light, nor darkness, Only the EXISTENT ONE breathed calmly self-contained. Naught else but he was there, naught else above, beyond."

Greece

The religion of Greece was originally monotheistic. Says Dr. Martin.

> "The Orphic hymns, long before the advent of the popular divinities, celebrated the Pantheos, the Universal God." (Quoted by Dr. Ellinwood, "Oriental Religions and Christianity," pg. 228.)

Babylon

Do we find traces of monotheism in Babylon? Hear Winkler:

> "There are many, nay numberless gods; but they are only revelation forms of the one great divine might." (Quoted by Orr, "Problems of Old Testament," pg. 409.)

China

Professor Legge, of Oxford, contends that at a still earlier period than the dynasty of Yao and Shun the worship of one God existed in China. He says:

> "Five thousand years ago the Chinese were monotheists—not henotheists, but monotheists." (The Religions of China, pg.

16.)

I have here the statements of men who are authorities in this field showing that the same is true of Arabia, Persia, Africa, and other nations. But time will not permit me to introduce these. However, I want before closing this line of evidence to show you that our position holds good with what is probably the lowest of any of the races extant:

Aborigines of Australia

Our earliest account of these people is from Dampier, who visited the country in 1688. He describes the natives as the "miserablest people in the world." They had no metals, bows, pottery, sheep, poultry, etc. They had no houses; their only dwelling-place was a fire with a few boughs before it. Yet even these people "believe in a Supreme Being whose abode is in the heavens, and who observes and rewards conduct." ("The Making of Religion," by Andrew Lang, M.A., LL.D., pg. 189, 194.)

I think every reasonable person here will say that I have shown conclusively that all over the earth, wherever human beings are found, they are religious; that regardless of how low in the scale of civilization they may have fallen, there is still to be found a trace of the worship of one God; that the earliest stages of all religions are the purest stages. There are many points of similarity between these various religions and the further back we go the more alike do we find them. Listen to this quotation from a man who was selected by some thirty of the best scholars in America, to lecture on the History of Religions:

> "Look in what continent we please, we shall find the myth of a Creation or of a primeval construction, of a Deluge or a destruction, and of an expected Restoration." (Daniel G. Brinton, A.M., M.D., LL.D., Sc.D., Professor of American Archaeology and Linguistics, University of Pennsylvania, in "Religions of Primitive Peoples," pg. 122.)

It seems to me that all these facts can point to but one conclusion: In the beginning of the human race the Supreme Being gave to his creature, man, a revelation of Himself. All the religions of earth are but corruptions of this original revelation. I challenge Mr. Smith to account for the facts we have shown in any other manner. If he cannot, then I urge upon him the inevitable conclusion that there is a Supreme Being, as is evidenced by the fact that each nation of the world bears testimony of His having spoken to man. I insist that we can account for these facts only in the language of the ancient Preacher:

> "God hath made man uprght, but they have sought out many inventions." (Eccl. 7:9).

Or in the language of the great Apostle:

> "Because that, when they knew God, they glorified him not as God, neither were thankful; but became vain in their imaginations, and their foolish heart was darkened; professing themselves to be wise, they became fools, and changed the glory of the incorruptible God into an image made like to corruptible man, and to birds, and four-footed beasts, and creeping things. Wherefore God also gave them up to uncleanness through the lusts of their own hearts, to dishonor their own bodies between themselves; Who change the truth of God into a lie, and worshipped and served the creature more than the Creator, who is blessed forever." (Rom. 1:21-25.)

DEDUCTIVE PROOF

In the process of deduction we reason from the general to the particular, from the universal to the individual. This method of reasoning is used extensively in the mathematical sciences—algebra, geometry, trigonometry, analytics, calculus, etc. We have certain ideas of time, space, motion, number etc. These ideas are perfectly clear in the sense in which we use them, and concerning them we are able to affirm some universal principles. Starting with these principles which we consider axiomatic, we travel far and wide, building up a great system of truth. "Things which are equal to each other are equal to the same thing" is an axiom accepted by all mathematicians. Another mathematical axiom is that "a straight line is the shortest distance between two points." Another is that "the whole is equal to the sum of all the parts." We accept these statements as being self-evident; they do not require any proof. Who can prove these axioms by formal logic? The human mind is so constructed that it does not require proof of the self-evident. Some things must be taken for granted in all sound systems of final research. Most of our conclusions in mathematics relate back to the self-evident—that for which the mind asked no proof.

Now I wish to apply these principles of deductive reasoning to the proof of the existence of God. I maintain that in this field there are truths that are as self-evident as the axioms of mathematics. One of these axioms I ask my opponent to consider is this

"Something cannot come from nothing."

Such a truth as this needs no proof, the intelligent man accepts it as prima fade. Now let us consider another:

"Something is (exists)."

This too, is self-evident. Now I ask you to consider this syllogism

"Something cannot come from nothing; but something is; therefore something always was."

Let us change the wording, but not the meaning:

"Something cannot create itself, but something is created; therefore, something was always created, or was self-existent."

Now I ask my opponent to name that "something" that always was. What is it that is self-existent, eternal? The Christian says that something is God. If that something is not God, let Mr. Smith tell us what it is.

Let us continue this line of reasoning a little farther

"A like cause must produce a like effect."

If a cause produced an effect greater than itself, this would be equivalent to something coming from nothing. Now notice our minor premise:

"Rational (thinking) being exists."

This is self-evident. Descartes, one of the fathers of modern philosophy, tried to doubt everything, but was finally forced to a belief in his own existence. From this he formed his famous axiom:

"I think, therefore I am."

We cannot reasonably question the existence of thinking beings. But, rational being cannot come from irrational being; the unthinking cannot produce the thinking. If this were possible, we would again have something produced by nothing. With these truths established, let us consider their application.

"Thinking being exists, but thinking being could not come from unthinking being; therefore, thinking being has always existed."

Now I ask my opponent to tell us what this eternal, rational, or thinking being is. We say it is God. What alternative has my opponent to offer?

INDUCTIVE PROOF

In the process of inductive reasoning the mind begins with the particular and proceeds to the general. This is the method of the scientist. The greater part of our knowledge is gained through this method of mental activity. Inductively, we argue the existence of God from the things about which we know. Paul reasons in this way in Romans 1:19, 20:

"Because that which may be known of God is manifest in them; for God hath showed it unto them. For the invisible things of Him from the creation of the world are clearly seen, being understood by the things that are made, even his eternal power and Godhead; so that they are without excuse."

It has been said that,

"If the word 'God' were written upon every blowing leaf, embossed on every passing cloud, engraved on every granite rock; the inductive evidence of God in the world would be no stronger than it is. When the human intellect thinks in terms of finality with the world as. its premise, the therefore of every syllogism is God. The universe is a big advertising poster that spells 'God.'" (E. A. Maness, B.L., M.A., Ph.D., in "Evidence of Divine Being." pg. 27.)

GRAVITATION

It has been estimated that if all the men who have lived on the earth during the past six thousand years were to put their combined strength against the earth, they could perhaps move it about a foot in a thousand years. Yet there is a force which moves this earth at the rate of more than a thousand miles a minute. What is this force? We call it gravitation. It is one of those things about which we talk much, and know little. This force moves our earth systematically and orderly, so that the seasons, as well as day and night, follow each other in regular order. Is this the result of blind chance? Can you see no intelligence in this operation? I am tempted to say that the man who can see no intelligence in this orderly, systematic program simply does not have intelligence enough to see it! Perhaps that is the trouble with the athe-ist.

This same force, which we call gravitation, is working constantly in the great domain of space about us. The planets do not move across the heavens in a haphazard, hit-or-miss manner; each planet moves in its particular orbit, and with almost clock-like precision. Because of this orderly procedure, astronomers are able to predict the exact date of an eclipse, or other planetary action. Because we have observed the systematic way in which gravity operates, we speak of the "law of gravitation." What is this law? Can there be a law without a law-maker? Who made the law of gravitation?

ASTRONOMY

The sweet Singer of Israel exclaimed

> "The heavens declare the glory of God, and *the firmament* showeth his handiwork." (Psa. 19:2.)

If you were to look into the skies on a clear night, under the most favorable circumstances, you should be able to see six or seven thousand stars. With the aid of the high-powered telescope we are able to count something like one hundred millions; photographic plates reveal hundreds of millions more than the telescope; and we have evidence that beyond these are countless myriads of planets and stars that we have never been able to discover. Our closest fixed star is probably Alpha, of the constellation of Centauri; yet, when we look at Alpha we are not seeing Alpha as she is today, but as she was almost five years ago, for it takes light—travelling at the tremendous speed of one hundred eighty-six thousand miles a second, nearly five years to come from Alpha to us. Thus we see that our nearest neighbor among the starry hosts is some twenty-five trillion miles away.

Pollus, the brighter star of the "Twins," is some twenty-four light-years distant from the earth. The term, "light-year" is used in astronomy as we use the expressions "a ten-minute walk" or a "two-hour drive." We use the time required in walking or driving as a unit of measurement. In actual miles, Pollux is approximately 145,000,000,000,000 miles away! Castor, the other "twin" is some twenty light-years farther than Pollux. We are now receiving its light-message of some fifty years ago. For a long time astronomers, depending upon the method of surveying by triangulation, could not calculate the distance to stars that are more than about three hundred light-years from us; the diameter of the earth was not sufficient for the imaginary triangle base. But now, through ingenious methods first developed at the Mount Wilson Observatory, they are able to calculate the distaike to any star or swarm of stars whose light can be caught by the most high-powered telescope.

The latest measurements of the universe, the work of Dr. Allen Douglas Maxwell, of the Lick Observatory on Mount Hamilton, have reached as far as fifteen thousand light years—one hundred quadrillion miles. In other words, the light that entered Dr. Maxwell's telescope and blackened the photographic plate, left the star fifteen thousand years before. And still the immensity of space goes on and on—how far, we cannot now know. What power must have been required to bring into existence such an immense universe! Certainly "the heavens declare the glory of God!"

The order in which these countless planets are found and the precision and harmony with which they move, are no less wonderful than the immense space which they occupy. Astronomers find that the stars are not sprinkled at random in space, but are grotiped together in countless universes. Some plan has been followed in their grouping; some intelligence has designed them. We contend that God designed and grouped them. What is the atheist's solution to the problem?

Dr. Charles Young, Professor of Astronomy, Princeton College, in his larger text book on astronomy, pg. 515, has this to say:

> "We see that our planetary system is not a mere accidental aggregation of bodies. Masses of matter coming haphazard towards the sun would move, as comets do, in orbits, always conic sections, to be sure, but of every degree of accentricity of inclination. There are a multitude of relations actually observed in the planetary system which are wholly independent of gravitation and demand explanation."

Dr. Young then enumerates eight of these "relations," which he says are independent of gravitation and demand explanation. If the atheist could explain gravitation—which he cannot, he would still have a "multitude of actually observed relations" to explain. I challenge Mr. Smith to offer any plausible explanation of these matters, without admitting a Supreme Intelligence!

The evidence of design is not limited to the big things of the universe. The most minute things bear evidence of having been designed. Do you know that every snowflake that falls upon the earth has an angle of sixty, or one hundred and twenty degrees? A great mathematician has said that "the heavens are but crystalized mathematics." I ask you who set the angles of the snowflake? With whose square and compasses were they designed? The atheist cannot explain so small a thing as a snowflake. The Christian can explain it in the one word, "God." My friend cannot explain it in a million words, without God. In fact, I challenge my opponent to explain anything, without God!

THE LAW OF PROBABILITIES

Mathematics deal with what is known as the Law of Probabilities. It has been calculated that if the twenty-six letters of the alphabet were tossed promiscuously into the air by chance force, they might fall together in the present order of the alphabet—A-B-C-etc., once in five hundred million, million, million times that they were thus tossed up and allowed to fall without guidance. I ask, on this basis, what would be the probability of the innumerable combinations of nature coming together in the wonderful order of the universe, iflhey were tossed about by blind chance? It would be just as reasonable to suppose that the letters of the alphabet, tossed about unintelligently, would form themselves into a learned treatise on science or philosophy. Certainly it is no more unreasonable to think that a book about the heavens could be formed by chance than to think that the heavens themselves are the result of chance.

I have heard that Kircher, the great astronomer, made a globe upon which he pictured the location of the planets. An atheistic friend noticed the globe, and exclaimed: "What a remarkable of workmanship! Who made it?" Keicher replied: "I do not know to whom it belongs, nor where it came from; but one thing I know, nobody made it." "What? That is impossible," contended the atheist, "Someone must have made it. Such a perfectly arranged globe could not have made itself." To which Kircher replied: "Nor could such a perfectly arranged universe--of which this is but a small representation —have made itself."

ENERGY

The same energy we find asserting itself in the operation of planets is also found to be working in the most minute things in the world. A microbe so small you cannot see it without the aid of a microscope, will produce in three or four hours something like a million more just like itself.

Speaking of energy, science tells us there is enough energy in every ounce of coal brought out, if properly used, to pull two tons a mile; and there are substances containing energy in a much more compressed form than it is in coal. Take radium; Dr. Millikan tells us that a gram of radium shoots off each second 145,000 billion particles (known as alpha particles), and that these particles reach the speed of twelve thousand miles a second. The beta rays travel more than ten times as fast as the alpha particles. The gamma rays are sent off at the rate of thirty billion billions per second. The helium atoms sent forth by radium shoot right through solids, as though nothing stood in the way. Radium contains 300,000 times more energy per gram than coal contains. ("Science and Life," by Dr. Robert A. Milliken).

The air is charged with waves in the ether; sounds travelling throughout the universe are now heard by means of the radio. Who can, without God, account for these remarkable energies all ceaselessly engaged in a most harmonious *and systematic* work?

LIFE

We have been accustomed to think of inorganic matter as dead; but it is now believed that *gases,* liquids and even solids are subject to radio-activity, in a state of constant change, electrons eternally jostling, moving and disturbing. The universe is alive; life is expressing itself from every source.

Can the atheist account for the origin of life? Is there any way to account for it, without *a* Supreme Life? I challenge Mr. Smith to offer us an account of life's beginning.

Science cannot solve the problem. Huxley says:

> "Of the causes which lead to the origin of living matter, it may be said that we know absolutely nothing." (Article on Biology in Encyclopedia Britannica.)

Professor Henry Fairfield Osborn, head of the American Museum of Natural History, says:

> "The mode of the origin of life is a matter of pure speculation in which we have as yet little observation or uniformitarian reasoning to guide us, for all the experiments of Butschli and others, to imitate the original life process, have proved fruitless." (The Origin and Evolution of Life, pg. 67.)

Darwin said:

> "The inquiry as to how life first originated is hopeless."

Professor Tyndall, after nearly a thousand experiments with organic infusions, concluded that,

> "Living things come only from the living."

Professor Dana, renowned geologist, gives this testimony:

> "Science has no explanation of the origin of life." (Manual of Geology.)

Jordan and Kellogg, in their book, "Evolution and Animal Life," page 41, make this statement:

> "Finally, we may refer briefly to the 'grand problem' of the origin of life itself. Any treatment of this question is bound to be wholly theoretical. We do not know a single thing about it. —All life comes from life. The biologist cannot admit spontaneous generation in the face of the scientific evidence he has."

We might continue indefinitely with such quotations from scientists. All agree that science does not solve the problem of life's origin. However, let us hear one more scholar. This man, Prof. H. W. Conn, of Wesleyan University, gives us no hope that science can ever answer the question. Listen to his testimony:

> "Upon this subject it must be confessed we are in as deep ignorance as ever. Indeed, if anything, the disclosures of the modern microscope have placed the solution of this problem *even* further from our grasp." (Method of Evolution.)

Science cannot tell us of the beginning of life, but it does give us the rule that "life comes only from life." In view of this truth, how can we account for life without a self-existent First Life? Let our atheist friend come forward with an answer to the question of life's origin—an answer that harmonizes with his Godless theory.

ATHEISM ACCOUNTS FOR NOTHING

Atheism cannot account for the origin of consciousness. If the beginning of life could be explained on a purely materialistic basis, there would still be the necessity of explaining the cause of conscious life.

Man has a moral nature not possessed by the beast. An animal shows no signs of compunction of conscience after having killed a fellow member of his species. Certain animals have been known to kill and eat their own offspring. Man has conscience. From whence did it come?

How do atheists explain the esthetic nature of man—the taste for music, the love of the beautiful? How could any "struggle for existence" have produced this? Even Huxley, though he claimed to be an agnostic, said:

> "One thing which weighs with me against pessimism and tells for a benevolent author of the universe, is my enjoyment of scenery and music. I do not see how they can have helped in the struggle for existence. They are gratuitous gifts." (Darwinism, pg. 478.)

In fact, atheism cannot account for anything. If there be no God, then, as someone has said:

> "Life is certainly a useless package, handed to us by some ruthless enemy."

Mr. Smith reminds me of the story of a dog on an express car (I am not comparing him to a dog, except as far as this story goes). Someone asked the man in charge of the express: "Where does this dog go?" 'The expressman answered: "I don't know, he don't know, nobody don't know; because he's gone and chewed up his tag." According to atheism, nobody knows where we came from, why we are here, or where we are going. We refuse to let the atheist "chew up the tag!"

I thank you, ladies and gentlemen.

Smith's First Reply

Mr. Chairman, Respected Opponent, Ladies and Gentlemen:

Inasmuch as the other side has specially asked that there be no applause, I make the same request. In speaking with my opponent this afternoon about the matter, I suggested that the audience be given no instructions. In Atheist meetings the audience takes part. You don't sit as dumb bells; you can express your opinion: when you go to a church you don't express your opinion; or if you do, they tell the police.

I want to say a word complimentary to my opponent and the pastor of this church. I have very little respect for their judgment, but a great deal for their courage. Unlike other ministers in this town they believe their doctrines can be defended in the open. Their fellow clergymen know better; they know that the Christian religion will not stand criticism and open debate.

Let me tell you something of how I came to be an Atheist. I used to live in Maud, Oklahoma—was there before the town was built; and have lived in Shawnee. I was in this town some twenty years ago, working for the Farmers' Union. I joined the First Methodist Church. A few years later, I went to a Methodist school, Epworth University, in Oklahoma City.

The following Summer I worked for the State Code Commission in Guthrie. One Saturday afternoon I found in the library a book entitled: "Jefferson's Bible." Being a Democrat, I greatly admired Jefferson. The book interested me. I found from reading the introduction to that book that Thomas Jefferson was an infidel. He did not believe that Jesus was the son of God; *he* thus ridiculed the virgin birth:

> "The day will come when the mystical generation of Jesus, by the Supreme Being as his father in the womb of a virgin, will be classed with the fable of the generation of Minerva in the brain of Jupiter." (Works v. 4, p. 365.)

That day has come. The preachers did not tell me that. Have they told you? They conceal such facts, and a great deal more. If *you* will investigate, you will find that the great men of this country, and our greatest Presidents, have not been Christians.

The next season I went to the State University at Norman. I tried to continue to believe the Christian religion, but began to investigate its doctrines. One day when watching a football game with my pastor, I asked him if he believed the virgin birth story, and the Adam and Eve story. He said, "Why, of course not." I demanded: "Why do you not tell your congregation that?" He replied: "That would do a great deal of harm, and no good."

I expect that in Shawnee you have such men among the ministers who oppose this debate. They will admit privately that they believe in evolution; yet, they preach a Savior, and that is why they endeavored to suppress this debate. The descendants of apes don't need a Savior. An evolutionist preaching Jesus crucified is in no position to appear in a public discussion.

I continued investigating, but still retained my faith and prayed daily. The time came when I realized there was nobody above listening to my words. I ceased to pray.

I found no stopping place short of atheism. I went East, and after years of study, with others in New York City, in 1925, launched the American Association for the Advancement of Atheism. We received a charter, and we are now duly incorporated under the Laws of the State of New York. Our headquarters are at 119 East Fourteenth

Street. You can look us up. You will find our charter in the State Capitol at Albany.

There is a great deal of prejudice against atheism. Thomas Jefferson said:

> "It does me no harm for my neighbor to say there are twenty gods or no god. It neither breaks my leg nor picks my pocket."

How many Christians have that attitude? A Roman emperor said:

> "Injuries to the gods, should be the concern of the gods."

Why don't we have that spirit of tolerance today? No, every little two-by-four preacher takes it upon himself to defend the ruler of the universe.

Last evening I made application to the town council in Maud to be granted equal privileges with a representative of the American Bible Society, who was selling religious literature on the streets. The mayor spoke feelingly of "The Holy Bible" and "Mother's religion." I lost out.

I noticed as I came in the door a motto, reading in part:

> "It is better to work with a construction gang than with the wrecking crew."

You are, in this city, tearing down and building all the time. Do you mean to say that men who do the wrecking are baser than the ones who build? The one is as necessary as the other. If you will look in the New York City directory under "Wrecking Companies," you will find some forty concerns listed. No one prosecutes them. The men who tear down condemned buildings are just as necessary as the men who build skyscrapers. The Christian religion has been condemned by the civilized conscience of the world, and our business is to wreck it.

The question is often asked, "What will you put in its place?" We don't put anything in its place. When a physician cures you of a, disease he does not give you another disease; he merely restores you to health. We seek to restore you to reason.

In the short time left, I shall give you briefly the arguments for atheism, refute some of the arguments for theism, and then introduce Dr. Sparkes Gladman, the great theologian of the atheistic movement.

Let us consider the origin of religion. My opponent is all mixed up when he says that monotheism degenerated into polytheism. It is not so taught even in the theological schools. The Fundamentalists of this country have lost control of almost every theological seminary. They will soon lose control of the Baptist Seminary in Louisville, Ky. They lost their last major school in the North this year when they lost Princeton Seminary.

No! Religion arose through error. Primitive man was unable to explain what he saw about him. I have not the time to give in detail the various factors in the evolution of religion. Primitive man, when he ate too much, had dreams and on awaking he recalled the dream and decided that he had been somewhere; and in this way he came to the idea that he had a spirit, had a soul that could leave his body. The beliefs in magic, animism, ghosts, and ancestor worship contributed to the growth of religion. In my judgment ancestor worship was the principal factor. As Grant Allen has well said:

"Corpse worship is the protoplasm of religion."

You cannot refine falsehood into truth.

Let us consider the five fundamentals of atheism. The first is Materialism, the doctrine that Matter, with its indwelling property, Force, constitutes the reality of the universe. In other words, there is no spirit, soul or supreme being. If I were to strike a match you would see a flame burst forth. If, I move the match suddenly or hold it long enough, the flame is said to go out. Where does it go? It does not go anywhere, because it never existed, except as matter in motion. The same is true of us.

There is no soul or free-will. Voltaire defined free-will as the faculty bestowed by the grace of God upon man whereby he may get himself damned.

The second fundamental of atheism is that which, for lack of a better word, we call Empiricism, or Sensationalism. It is the doctrine that all our knowledge is derived from experience. You have had no experience with God. You have no idea with which to form a conception of God. I know my opponent has contended—it has always been the contention of priests and preachers—that man has born within him a religious sense. The idea of God is innate, *says* the priest, and my opponent tells us tonight men everywhere believe in God. Yet, you find that the clergy are trying to inculcate the idea of God into every child. They are bootlegging their religion into our public schools. They know that every child is born an atheist.

Our third basic doctrine is that of Evolution, which will be debated tomorrow night.

Our fourth fundamental is Hedonism, the doctrine that happiness here and now should be the motive of conduct. That will come up tomorrow afternoon when we consider whether or not Christianity benefited mankind.

The last fundamental of atheism is the Existence of Evil. More than two thousand years ago, Epicurus bottled up God with logic forever in these words:

> "Either God wishes to destroy evil and cannot; or he can but will not; or neither wishes nor has the power; or he both desires and is able. If he wishes and cannot, he is impotent; if he can but will not, he is wicked; if he neither wishes nor can, he is impotent as well as wicked; if he can and will, why does evil exist?"

For two thousand years the priests have been unable to refute the Greek atheist. That which rules the universe knows no right or wrong. If a man gets cold and wet helping a friend in distress, the consequences to his health are the same as if he were committing murder. Perhaps in a thoughtless moment you have sung the Doxology, "Praise God from whom all blessings flow." It is as unreasonable as the New Doxology which we atheists sometimes sing, "Praise God from whom all cyclones blow." The Almighty God could, and a Heavenly Father would, prevent evil. There is something wrong. If there be a good God, why did he not arrange another way to perpetuate life than by having one animal eat another? Huxley says:

> "If our hearing were sufficiently acute to catch every note of

pain, we would be deafened by one continuous scream."

If there be a God who knows everything, he knows that life feeds upon life.

Sixty parasites prey upon man. Did God make them? If so, what do you think of him for having made them? Some of those parasites live only upon the body of man; and if they did not evolve, they were created in the beginning, and must have lived on Adam and Eve. They must have been the two most diseased persons that ever lived.

I believe prayer and providence are being given up except in the more backwoods sections of the country. Which portions of the world are most religious? You know it is the South—my own home land. But the South has always led the North in the commission of murder. Memphis, Tennessee, where there are no atheist societies and where evolution is outlawed, has led this country in murder for the last twenty years, with one or two exceptions, when pious Jacksonville, Florida, took the lead. A Fundamentalist in New-York recently declared that it is easier to convert negroes in the Congo to Christianity than to convert the professors at Columbia University. Of course, he was right. If you want to get people to believe in God, don't go to educated people; go to the hillbillies of Arkansas and the Hottentots in Africa.

In the old days, they prayed for rain. Why don't you have the Governor of this state set aside a day to pray that the drought may end? Crops are burning up; the cotton will soon suffer; and the corn that was not made some ten days ago is ruined. Formerly Christians prayed when they were sick. In St. James, last chapter, it says:

"Is any sick among you? Send for a physician."

No, that is what the atheist does. The Bible says:

"Call for the elders of the church; and let them pray over him, anointing him with oil in the name of the Lord; and the prayer of faith shall save the sick."

Who of you do that? Last night in Maud I heard an old woman, a true Christian, lament that many who call themselves Christians, the moment they get sick, send for a physician.

If there is a being who controls the universe, what do you think of his system of raising fruit in Oklahoma? When I was a boy living at Maud, every Spring I saw with joy, the fruit trees in bloom, expecting to have lots of apples and peaches to eat; but four times out of five, frost came so late that the fruit was killed. Four times out of five that happens in Oklahoma. Is that good management?

You have a theologian in this city by the name of Vanderpool. I read one of his sermons. He says that when a great man is needed God always sends him. In the middle ages for a thousand years schools were almost blotted from the face of the earth. Humanity was in darkness, because religion stopped the development of science. Instead of following the Greeks in treating disease, the Christians followed Jesus and Paul who believed the insane were possessed by demons. Christianity caused the Dark Ages. Why did not God send someone during that period? Andrew Carnegie, who has done more to disseminate knowledge than any other American, through establishing libraries (he built one in this city) said:

> "I have not bothered Providence with my petitions for about forty years."

Only the other day I read a significant item in a magazine called "Liberty," which has a circulation of over two million copies (I give this as an illustration of the trend of the times—as showing that belief in prayer and providence is being abandoned in the enlightened centers). Liberty is published in Chicago by the same concern publishing The Chicago Tribune. They are giving $5.00 for every bright saying of a child which they accept. One mother sent in this saying, which was printed.

You will see that her child asked a question that my friend here cannot answer. A preacher discoursing concerning a certain disaster at sea, said five thousand passengers were providentially saved. The girl asked the preacher how many were providentially drowned.

There was a 17th Century bishop in England by the name of Hall who preached providence. This bishop endeavored to prove the existence of a watchful Heavenly Father by citing a certain incident in his life. He started on a trip overseas, when, by the interposition of providence, he was just prevented from boarding the ship which later sank with all on board. How about the others? To be religious, you must practice the art of ignoring.

If prayer ever accomplished anything, why did the World War continue? This Dr. Gladman, of whom I spoke in the beginning, says prayer is answered when God is awake, but that he sometimes sleeps. During the War all preachers prayed for *peace,* and I dare say my opponent in his church in Dallas prayed for peace. Dr. Gladman says that the moment God woke up the war ended.

It may be that as children in school, you read the poem by Bryant entitled, "To a Water Fowl."

"He who from zone to zone guides thy boundless flight, In the long way that I must tread alone, Will guide my steps aright."

That poet may have eaten that very bird for dinner that evening, after writing that poem.

My opponent has discoursed to you very eloquently about snowflakes, about their angles, and how God must have squared them off. If God made everything, including snowflakes, he must have made disease germs, the germs of small pox and syphilis, and of diptheria that kills children. Why did not my opponent speak of that? The clergy like to talk about the human eye, and how it could not have happened by chance. If God made good eyes, who made cross eyes, blear eyes, and squint eyes? Why not talk of the fangs of the rattlesnake? Don't they fulfill their functions? You cannot believe in a good God, unless you have a double standard of morals, one for man and another for God. If you have the same standard of morals for both, God stands condemned before the bar of human reason.

A few years ago in Arizona a mother and child were left alone on a ranch. The father had gone away. A rattlesnake bit the mother. She tried to get help, but was far distant from the nearest human being. What could she do? She saw she was *going* to die and that the children would starve, as the father would not return for a week. She killed her babies and herself. How can you explain such an event if God exists? If you could have helped that woman, would you not have helped her? Maybe you Christians will say that she forgot to pray. If God must be begged before he will help, is he worthy of worship?

Here is another question. You who believe in God, if you don't like this answer, give us a better one: "Why does not God reveal a cure for cancer?" The answer: "He will, when scientists discover it. That is his method. He prefers to share the credit with others rather than hog all the glory himself." Voltaire, who did more to liberate the human race than any other man, said that prayer and arsenic will kill a cow.

A man asked this question: "I long for the consolations of religion, but my reason forbids. Would you suggest a surgical operation to weaken my mind?" Dr. Gladman counseled: "No, that is not necessary, go to church regularly, cease to reason, and exercise the faculty of faith; and you will probably get relief. If these means are unsuccessful, time will help you out. As you grow old, you will become sufficiently feebleminded to accept religion."

One man says he has found a pocket book containing a considerable sum of money and wants to know whether or not he should give thanks to God. The answer is that he should, especially as God will probably receive no thanks from the person who lost the pocketbook.

In conclusion, let me introduce you to Dr. Sparkes Gladman, the most eminent theologian of the United States, the present company, Rev. Oliphant, and Rev. Cullum, excepted. This is the *way* he answers the questions, and if these are not correct, I ask my opponent to give the right answer. "Who made God?" The answer is, "Like most persons who have amounted to anything, God is self-made. He made himself out of nothing just prior to the beginning. The act of self-creation—the greatest miracle of all time—ought to convince even an atheist."

Oliphant's Second Affirmative

(Duration, 20 minutes)

Brother Chairman, Ladies and Gentlemen, Respected Opponent:

I am wondering if I have been misinformed about the rules of controversy. I have been taught that it is the duty of a speaker on the negative side of a proposition to consider and attempt to refute the arguments made by the, affirmative. But I must confess that if the speech to which you have just listened is to be considered the standard, I have had the wrong idea. Mr. Smith scarcely referred, directly or indirectly, to my speech. In my opening speech I made a number of arguments which I consider germane to the issue. It seems to me that my opponent should have made an effort to refute these arguments, or attempted to show that they are foreign to the question under consideration. How many of my arguments did he attempt to answer? (Here the speaker was interrupted by an atheist in the audience who said: "I can answer three of your arguments.") Mr. Oliphant: I thank the gentleman for his admission that he can answer only three of the many arguments I presented. What about the others? Sir, are you dissatisfied with the work of the president of your association? I do not blame you. If I were in your place I should be dissatisfied, too. However, if when this debate is over, you think Mr. Smith has not done justice to your cause, I shall be glad to give you a chance to see if you can do a better job.

Now to continue my speech. It is not primarily my duty to answer the arguments of the negative. However, I shall consider everything the gentleman says, that is at all worthy of notice. Some of his statements are so childish that my ten-year-old daughter could answer them.

What Mr. Smith *says* about Modernist preachers knowing that their doctrine will not bear the test of public discussion, may be true. I have no desire to defend them. I am content to present the truth of God's word, and leave those who hear to decide whether it stands the test.

My opponent tells us "how he came to be an atheist." I am not particularly interested in that. His faith was shaken by a preacher who did not believe the Bible. For a man who does not believe God's word to pretend to preach it is a travesty on common decency. Mr. Smith should not be influenced so easily by preachers. He should think for himself. However, if an unbelieving preacher could lead him away from faith in God, possibly I can lead him back.

Mr. Smith intimates that Thomas Jefferson had a part in making him an atheist. Jefferson was not an atheist. Hear him:

> "The rights of conscience we never submitted we could not submit. We are answerable to them to our God." (Notes on Virginia, 1782, F. 111, 264.)

In his bill for establishing religious freedom, Mr. Jefferson said:

> "Almighty God hath created the mind free and manifested his supreme will that free it shall remain by making it altogether insusceptible of restraint—" (1779, F. 11, 238.)

Hear him once more as he plainly declares:

> "An atheist I can never be." (Letter to John Adams. Quoted by Wm. E. Curtis, in "The True Thomas Jefferson," pg. 309.)

Mr. Jefferson referred to the so-called "Jefferson Bible," of which Mr. Smith spoke, as:

"The Philosophy of Jesus of Nazareth, extracted from the account of his life and doctrines, as given by Matthew, Mark, Luke and John; being an abridgement of the New Testament for the use of the Indians, unembarrassed with matters of fact or faith beyond the level of their comprehension." (Preface, "Jefferson's Bible," published by N. D. Thompson Publishing Company.)

The fact that a certain city leads in the commission of crime does not prove that religion causes crime, unless it can be shown that the difference between this and other cities consists solely in a difference in degree of religiousness. Hundreds of other elements of difference may enter into the question.

Our friend tells us that the greatest presidents of the United States have been disbelievers. His statement is not true. All of our presidents (with two exceptions) have been members of some church. The exceptions are Lincoln and Jefferson. Lincoln was a very religious man and Jefferson was far from being an atheist.

The assertion that the most educated people of this country are disbelievers is about as near the truth as the statement about our presidents. A document expressing belief in God was, published in 1923. The following scientists signed the statement:

Charles D. Walcott, Geologist, President of the National Academy of Sciences, President of the American Association for the Advancement of Science, and Head of the Smithsonian Institute of Washington.

Henry Fairfield Osborn, Paleontologist, President of the American Museum of Natural History, New York.

Edwin Grant Conklin, Zoologist, Head of the Department of Zoology, Princeton University.

James Rowland Angell, Psychologist, President of Yale University.

John Merle Coulter, Botanist, Head of the Department of Botany, University of Chicago.

Michael I. Pugin, Physcist and Engineer, Professor of Electromechanics and Director of Phoenix Research Laboratory, Columbia University.

William James Mayo, Surgeon, Mayo Foundation for Medical Education and Research, Rochester, Minnesota.

George David Berkhoff, Mathematician, Head of the Department of Mathematics, Harvard University, Cambridge, Massachusetts.

Arthur A. Noyes, Chemist, Director of the Gates Chemical Laboratory, California Institute of Technology, Pasadena, California.

William Wallace Campbell, Astronomer Director of Lick Observatory and President-elect of the University of California.

John J. Carthy, Engineer, Vice-President in Charge of Research, American Telephone and Telegraph Company, New York.

Robert A. Milliken, Physicist, Director of Norman Bridge Laboratory of Physics, Pasadena, California.

William Henry Welch, Pathologist, Director of the School of Hygiene and Public Health, John Hopkins University, Baltimore.

John G. Merriam, Paleontologist, President of the Carnegie Institution of Washington.

Gano Dunn, Engineer, Chairman of the National Research Council, Washington, D. C.

The statement was also signed by a number of the leading business men of America, including Hon. Herbert Hoover, then Secretary of Commerce. Mr. Smith says these men are ignorant!

As a further refutation of the charge that religion and education do not go together, I ask you to examine the history of the great educational institutions of Europe and America. The University of Leyden was founded by a group of Christian Hollanders more than three hundred years ago. An examination of a list of twenty universities which were established in Europe between 1550 A.D. and 1700 A.D. shows that they were all founded and maintained by religious organizations.

The great universities of America were built by religious men. Harvard University was founded by the Puritans. Its first private benefactor was a preacher—John Harvard, from whom the institution received its name. Dr. James Blair (another preacher) was active in founding William and Mary College, and was first president of the school.

Where are the schools that atheists have built? I say, without fear of successful contradiction, that every educational institution in the world is—directly or indirectly—the fruit of religion. Let Mr. Smith name an exception. Atheists have never built a school or a hospital. Atheism offers nothing constructive. It has no standard. What do you have to believe to be an atheist? Nothing. What do you have to do to be an atheist? Nothing. What do you have to be to be an atheist? Nothing. Atheism sets no standard for belief, action or character.

Mr. Smith admits that he offers nothing constructive; he says he belongs to the "wrecking crew." He then compares atheism to the wrecking companies that wreck condemned buildings. Let me remind him that these companies wreck only buildings that have been condemned by proper authorities, or whose owners want them wrecked. Sir, Christians have not asked you to wreck their building, nor has the building been condemned by any legitimate authority. By whose authority are you making your feeble effort to wreck the building of God? If a wrecking company should wreck your home without proper authority, you would have them arrested. That's what they did to you over in Arkansas. My friends, it is not difficult to understand why he has such dislike for Arkansas. He was put in jail for his blasphemous attack on Christianity in that State.

Mr. Smith admits that atheism has nothing to offer in the place of Christianity. In an attempt to justify his wholly destructive doctrine, he says that when the doctor has removed disease, he does not give you anything to take its place. But the doctor does not attempt to remove anything that is beneficial to man. The atheist must first show us that religion is a disease. I have never seen a doctor out trying to convince healthy, happy people that they are sick, and should have disease removed. If the atheist is a doctor he is visiting well patients, and that without an invitation!

The wise doctor gives God credit for the healing of disease, through the wonderful curative powers of nature. I recently saw, over the office door of a Dallas physician, these words:

"We dress the wound, God heals it."

It is charged that religion arose through superstition, fetishism, animism, magic, etc. What proof does he offer? Merely his assertion. A man who will not accept the statements of Almighty God should not ask an intelligent audience to accept his bare assertions. In my first speech, I offered conclusive proof that all religions are but corrupted forms of the pure religion that God gave in the beginning. Mr. Smith answers this proof with an unsupported assertion!

The match and flame illustration means nothing for atheism until we are shown how a match can make and strike itself.

The question of whether man is a machine, without free will, belongs in tomorrow afternoon's discussion. It will be considered then.

Mr. Smith defines Empiricism (the second fundamental of atheism): "the doctrine that all our knowledge is derived from experience." He then argues that man has had no experience with God, and therefore, can have no conception of God. Well, let's try his own logic. Man can have no conception of God without experience with Him. But man, everywhere, has a conception of God. Therefore, man has had experience with God. It seems to me that our friend's premises (if true) point to the wrong conclusion for him. If man must have material with which to form a conception of anything, and he has formed a conception of God; does that not prove that man has such material as is necessary for such conception?

We all admit that there is evil in the world; but we cannot consistently blame God for it. Man has brought evil upon himself. Disease was brought into the world by sin. Had man lived in harmony with the law of God, there would have been no disease.

We are asked: "Why does God allow man to sin?" God has given man the power to think and act upon his own volition. If man chooses to act contrary to the laws of God, as revealed in His word and nature, God should not be considered responsible for the results. There could be but one way to be assured that man will not ˉsin; that is, make him a machine—with no power to govern his own actions. This would not be good for man. A mechanically perfect world would be very imperfect for man. Despite the terrible results of sin, who wants to give up his freedom of thought and action, to avoid the possibility of wrong-doing? I know that eating certain things will make me sick, but I do not want to give up my freedom of choice to avoid the possibility of illness. God has given certain laws governing man's health. Disobedience of these laws brings suffering. A law is of no value unless it provides a penalty for its violation.

Man could never be safe were it not for the fact that God governs the elements of nature by specific laws. What a terrible thing electricity would be, if not controlled by law! Man would indeed, be helpless, were it not that he can learn the laws of nature, and use them in furthering the interests of mankind. God has given certain laws in nature; and has given man intelligence, to be used in learning and using these laws. Man, living among the elements of a lawless nature, would have no use for intelligence.

The improper use of beneficial things may make them injurious. It is God's law in nature that fire will burn. If I put my hand in the fire, I must suffer the consequences; but God is not responsible for my suffering.

Evil is often the result of man's shutting out the good. The French Naturalist, Fabre, performed an experiment for the enlightenment of some boys. He put, a bird under a bell-glass from which the oxygen had been exhausted. Of course, the little creature was soon dead. The boys asked what was in the glass, and were told "nitrogen only." "What a terrible poison this nitrogen must be!" they exclaimed. "Not at all," said Fabre, "nitrogen is in the air we all breathe, and it does us no harm."

He then explained that it was not the presence of the nitrogen—but the absence of the oxygen that killed the bird. In the same way, evil may be the absence of God, hence, not "created" by Him. Then, that which we conceive to be evil may not, in its final analysis, be evil at all. Because of our limited vision, there are many things we cannot explain. A man who is inside a house (and has never been outside) cannot describe the house. We should not expect to describe the world and explain all its phenomena—being on the "inside," and having never been "outside."

The trouble with the atheist is that he considers himself the supreme judge of good and evil. How can man, with his circumscribed view of life, know what is good for a universe throughout eternity? Man's view of both time and space is *very* much limited. He should not attempt to sit in judgment on the word of God—at least not until he knows all the facts in the case!

We do not contend that God made all things just as they now exist. Two harmless medicines may, when mixed, become a deadly poison. Who knows but that disease germs may be the result of man's improper mixing of things, which as they were created, are good?

I was amused at Mr. Smith's remarks about this being a "backwoods" section of the country. He used to live here; but of course all the country's intelligence left with him! My only answer to this charge is that some boys can go to town and keep their equilibrium, while others cannot—and he seems to be one of the "others."

I am under no obligation to defend the foolish assertions attributed to this atheist dummy. Mr. Smith finds it easier to debate with a straw man of his own *making* than with a living opponent. Instead of resorting to "Dr. Gladman's" silly answer to the question; "Who made God?"—why did not Mr. Smith notice the arguments in my first speech which prove that God is an eternal, self-existent Being? The atheist assumes that something is eternal—why not God?

We are asked why God does not cure cancer. Perhaps God has given a remedy. Man is able to cure disease just to the extent that he discovers and uses God's remedies. God works through human instrumentality. A pessimist said: "I could make a better world than this." An optimist replied: "Well, let's go to work and do it." Man is given the power to either improve or degrade the world.

But we are told that man must do all the work and give God the credit.

Man cannot accomplish anything without the help of God. In whatever man undertake; he must have God's materials with which to work. What could man do without sunlight, or without air? Man is a very dependent creature; there is nothing he can do without the aid of elements which he cannot make for himself. Man certainly owes thanks to some one; and until Mr. Smith shows us that the blessings of nature are not the gift of God, we shall continue to thank God for them.

It is the rankest sort of egotism—the most contemptible type of self-exaltation, to set one's self up as being independent of the assistance of Divinity. Atheism begets egotism. Mr. Smith says in one of his tracts (describing this and another of his leaflets):

"The greatest anti-religious tracts ever written."

Of course he considers anti-religionists more intelligent than others; and now he just breaks down and confesses that he is the smartest disbeliever of all time! Such an attitude is to be expected of one who KNOWS there is no God!

In regard to "Dr. Gladman's" advice to his inquirer, that he go to church to weaken his mind: May I suggest that this is not the atheist's trouble.

What he needs is a religion weak enough for his feeble mind. I realize this is foolishness, but I am following my opponent—even when he introduces things which cannot be seriously considered.

My time has expired. I thank you for your attention.

Smith's Second Reply

Mr. Chairman, Respected Opponent, Ladies and Gentlemen:

My opponent accuses me of not having answered a single argument. Those of you who applauded must be deaf. He spoke of the wonderful design in the snowflake, and I asked you and him whether God designed the fangs of the rattlesnake; J could stand here all night and name things harmful to man. Did God make them?

The Rev. Oliphant would give you the impression that I said Jefferson was an atheist. I did not say it. I said he was "an infidel." Whoever says that he was a Christian says that which is not so. Jefferson called himself a materialist. He did not believe in the supernatural. He did not pray. They asked him to set aside a day for prayer. He refused to do it. He spoke of the doctrine of the Trinity as

> "The incomprehensible jargon of Trinitarian arithmetic, that three are one and one is three."

I will read something else by Jefferson. You will find this in his works, Vol. 4, page 325. He pronounces the Bible God "a being of terrific character, cruel, vindictive, capricious, and unjust." I did not say that Jefferson made me an atheist but that he was the first to set me investigating.

My friend *says* he cannot comprehend God nor explain him, but compares him to electricity. Electricity is not a substance any more than heat is a substance. It does not exist by itself. He *says* you cannot feel electricity. If you get hold of a live wire you will feel it as much as you feel heat. Does he hold that heat exists by itself? He further says that hope cannot be seen, and motherly love cannot be seen, but that they exist. Is that not really childish? Is mother-love a substance? You know it does not exist apart from mothers. My opponent is like a man who loves woman but hates each particular woman. He confuses the categories of existence. Preachers do not think clearly.

Some twenty years ago I was in New Orleans. Wandering one evening on the outskirts of the city, I came across a negro revival meeting. Sometimes the preacher did not talk sense—just one stream of words, without subjects and predicates. That did not bother his hearers. They were religious. Whenever he would say "Jesus," "salvation," and "heaven," they would shout, "hallelujah," "Glory to God," and "amen." Every preacher does the same thing. The clergy use words for their emotional value. I could take every sermon preached in this city last Sunday, including the one preached here, and put in the word "not" in every sentence and preach it, and if I kept a pious face, the congregation would not know the difference. They would come up and shake my hand and say, "Brother Smith, you certainly did preach a soul-searching sermon," and invite me home for a chicken dinner.

The Rev. Oliphant says that he has patience with the agnostic but none with the atheist who says there is no God. It may be some of the agnostics with whom he has patience are present. Let me say to them: If your position is such that you cannot come out in the open, go ahead as you are. You have our sympathy. You say you don't know whether or not there is a God. How do you know there are no witches? Almost invariably, if you ask an agnostic if there are witches, he will say no. Theological schools should have a "witchological" department.

My opponent says man everywhere has believed in God. He quotes me as saying you cannot form an idea without experience, and he says all men have an idea of God, therefore they must have had experience with God. He has changed ideas and conceptions until you don't know whom you are. I admit that the belief in God is widespread. It is not true, however, that there are no races without the belief. Some have had no conception of God. The belief in witches and evil spirits, however, is wider spread than the belief in God.' John Wesley said:

> "Giving up witchcraft is, in effect, giving up the Bible." (Journal, 1768.)

The Bible God commands:

> "Suffer not a witch to live."

Atheists came along and discredited the belief which caused hundreds of thousands of people to be put to death. During the period of witchcraft persecution, man came nearest to the God who created a hell where millions suffer throughout eternity. The preachers say that the teachings of the Bible were misinterpreted. God must be a poor inspirer if he so words his message that it is easily misunderstood.

My opponent has strange views concerning the development of religion. It seems he has never studied comparative religion. Long before Jehovah was known, the Jews and other races believed in many gods. Long before Adam and Eve there were men in different parts of the world who worshipped the sun. If you must worship, worship the sun—it is the true source of life.

My clerical opponent states that we cannot explain anything in a million words without God, but that Christians explain everything in one word—God. I don't know what your reaction is to that, but it sounds as absurd to me as would the advice of a fool who when you are trying to solve a problem comes along and says that all you have to do is put an X in the middle.

Holbach defined theology as "systematized ignorance." Epicurus declared:

> "God dwells in the inter-spaces of our knowledge of the world."

The more you learn, the more God recedes. There was a time when God was in medicine, but they don't resort to supernatural means now. God was in law. The priests ran the whole show. Priests are not holding their own in number or quality. There is a shortage of preachers. Empty churches are found all over the country.

The Rev. Oliphant endeavors to refute the argument that the soul is to the body as the flame is to the match, by asking "Did the match strike itself? It is a question he should not have asked, because spontaneous combustion does occur. Hay and grain under certain conditions burst into flame. I believe life originated in the same manner.

Thomas H. Huxley declared:

> "If the hypothesis of Evolution is true, living matter must have originated from non-living matter, for, by the hypothesis, the condition of the globe was at one time such that living matter could not have existed in it, life being entirely incompatible with the gaseous state."

Tyndall said:

> "If it were given to me to look beyond the abyss of geologically recorded time, to the still more remote period when the earth was passing through physical and chemical conditions which it can no more see again than a man can recall his infancy, I should expect to be a witness of the evolution of living protoplasm from non-living matter."

Again:

> "Evolution is a theory that not alone the lower forms of animal life—not alone the noble forms of the horse and the lion—not alone the wonderful mechanism of the human body, but the mind itself—emotion, intelligence, and will—were once latent in a fiery cloud. All our philosophy, science, and art were potential in the fires of the sun."

Synthetic chemistry has built up materials such as alcohol, which were once thought to be producible only by the vital activity of plants and animals. The creation of life by chemists in the laboratory would cause no great excitement. It is expected.

I believe in spontaneous generation. It is an essential of evolution. Prof. Alphonse Herrera of Mexico City, a member of our Association, has produced in the laboratory substances that behave much as does that which we call life. Scientists have produced some of the lower forms of life without crossing the two sexes. They have combined the germ cells of one sex with a chemical and it has produced life without the aid of the other sex.

My clerical friend is very oratorical about the wonders of the universe. He states that the planets keep perfect time. That sounds all right, unless you stop to think. Do the planets keep time? Yes, the sun always crosses the heavens in the day time and never at midnight. It is indeed remarkable. Don't you see what my friend is doing? He is putting the cart before the horse. You don't get anywhere by saying that each day is just twenty-four hours long. These are man-made measurements. Would I not be silly if I tried to prove to you there is a God because every foot contains twelve inches, never more nor less?

He said there were myriads of stars. Read the book called the Bible, and you will find that these innumerable stars, some of which are millions of times larger than this earth, are unimportant. We read:

"He made the stars also."

According to the scripture writer the stars were only an afterthought, and the earth was the big thing.

God's word says that the moon was made to rule the night. Half the time it appears during the day. It must not obey orders, or there would be no moonless nights.

The Vote of the Audience

Mr. Smith insisted that the audience be asked to vote on this proposition. Mr. Oliphant objected. It was his contention that questions of truth are not determined by majority vote. After some discussion, Mr. Oliphant consented to the questions being submitted to a vote. Mr. F. L. Paisley, chairman of the meeting, said: "All who believe that the affirmative speaker (Brother Oliphant) WON this discussion will please stand." Almost everyone in the audience stood. Mr. Paisley said: "I will not attempt to count this vast number. You may be seated. All those who think the negative speaker (Mr. Smith) won the debate will now rise to their feet." Seven persons stood.

The audience was dismissed with prayer, lead by Brother Will J. Cullum.

Atheist Morality vs. Christian Morality

(Friday afternoon, Aug. 16, 1929)

Proposition:

"Atheism is Beneficial to the Race, and is Most Conducive to Morality of any Theory Known to Man."

Affirmative: Charles Smith.
Negative: W. L. Oliphant.

Chairman, F. L. Paisley.

Smith's First Affirmative

Mr. Chairman, Ladies and Gentlemen, Honored Opponent:

The question for debate this afternoon is whether or not religion is necessary to support morals. Down through the centuries the priests and clergy have contended that unless you believe in God you cannot be good. That doctrine is what we atheists call the "morality lie." The truth is, nothing so deadens the moral conscience as religion. There is a story of a young lady who visited a seaport and while riding with a captain, asked: "What do the people of this town eat?" The captain replied, "Mostly fish." The young lady continued, "I thought fish was a brain food, and these seem to be the most stupid people I ever saw." He responded: "Imagine how they would look if they did not eat fish." The clergy tell us religion is what makes Christians moral, and when we point out that they exceed others in immorality, they tell us how immoral they would be if they had no religion!

Religion and crime, generally speaking, go together. Whether you take the people by classes or by sections, you will find that to be true. What section of the United States is the most religious? The South. It is known as the "Bible belt." In proportion to population, there are more murders in the South than any other section of the country. As I told you last night, the City of Memphis, Tennessee, leads the country in murders. The City of Little Rock is near the front in murder and piety. Which class of people are most given to crime? Is it the group of college professors, most of whom are atheists? They may not use the word "atheist," but they have no God, and they are atheists. Are they given to crime? No, not so much as the lower classes of people, intellectually speaking. You know it is the uneducated who are the most religious, and are most criminal. There are more religious than non-religious people in jail. In Sing Sing, according to the report for 1926, issued by Warden Lawes, 99 percent are religious—almost no atheists in that institution. We have a book entitled "Religion and Roguery," wherein are collected the statistics from the various prisons of the country, proving that religion and crime, generally speaking, go together. You know that Jesse James was much interested in theology, and believed in God. If this doctrine that these preachers give you be true—that accepting Jesus as your Savior insures your eternal happiness in heaven—be assured that most murderers hereafter will be happy, for they accept God and Jesus at the last moment. It was a consideration of these facts that caused Mark Twain, an atheist, to ex- claim:

"Heaven for climate; hell for company!"

Did you ever hear of the "Mann Act"—the Federal White Slave Law prohibiting the transportation across State lines of human beings for immoral purposes? It should be called the "Preachers' Act;" it catches so many wearers of the cloth. What is the explanation of the high criminality of the religious, and the high religiousness of criminals? Let my opponent explain why crime and religion go together. I hope he will not *give* the explanation given by a Georgia preacher, who stated that the clergy consume so much of their energy preaching morality as to have but little left with which to practice it.

I will give you the explanation. What causes a man to be a criminal, especially to commit violent crimes? It is an excess of emotional nature over reasoning power. That is the very thing that causes man to be religious. A thoroughly rational man does not act mad and shoot someone to get vengeance. Religion does not directly cause crime, except when some poor ignoramus has no better sense than to take certain parts of the Bible literally, and sacrifices a child, after reading in the Old Testament that human beings were sacrificed to God. That which causes religion causes crime. That is why they go together.

You heard the statement last evening that an atheist never built hospitals or established schools. If you are a preacher, you can make statements without having to prove them. If in a church, you ask questions, they call the police. If you go to an atheist meeting you can ask questions. Atheists have founded hospitals. No Bible-following Christian ever founded a hospital. You read in. James, 5th Chapter:

> "Is any sick among you, send him to a hospital."

No.

> "Send for the elders of the church, let them anoint him in the name of the Lord and the prayer of the faithful shall heal the sick."

That is the Bible doctrine of healing; and you will find how they cured insane persons by casting devils out of them. For two thousand years after Christ there were no insane asylums. They thought that those unbalanced mentally were possessed by devils; and that they should beat the devils out of these poor unfortunate persons.

My opponent last night referred especially to Harvard University, which I attended. He said it was founded by Christians. Yes, it is true Christians have founded most of the large educational institutions in the country. Atheists did not found them. Why? Up until the time the organization of which I have the honor to be President, was launched, were there any avowed atheists in this country? You know of your own knowledge that, with few exceptions, there were no atheists who called themselves that name. A man may have called another man an atheist; but the man himself did not use the title, because of the bigotry of the Christians.

It is not true that atheists never established colleges. What did Christians do when they were in power? They closed the schools of Athens, and for one thousand years humanity was in ignorance and darkness. Science and reason were outlawed. The Christians burned heretics at the stake. Spiritualism was supreme; materialism was rejected.

I shall now examine "Christian morality," and show you what a fraud it is. It is based on hope and fear—a system of threats and bribes. Heine, the German poet, asked:

> "Do you want a tip because you did not poison your brother and because you took care of your aged mother?"

That is what you Christians want. You want a reward for being good. I will read you a passage from the pagan writer:

> "Do good, for good is good to do; spurn bribe of heaven and threat of hell."

The Christian religion is profoundly immoral. The doctrine of atonement is barbarous. What is it? The innocent suffers for the guilty. An enraged God would not be at peace with us until an innocent person was put to death. Is there a mother or father who, if their child did wrong, and another child came to be whipped for the one who did the wrong, would whip that innocent child? Yet, that is what the preachers tell us God Almighty did.

Let me show you something of the immorality of the Bible. God established slavery. Read Lev. 25:44. Who was it that abolished slavery in modern times? It was the French Revolutionists. I quote from a man who should be listened to in this church. You have heard of the Rev. Alexander Campbell. I read you his words on the subject of slavery:

> "There is not one verse in the Bible inhibiting slavery, but many regulating it."

The founder of the Christian Church said slavery is not immoral according to the Bible, and he is right. God established it.

> "Thou shall not suffer a witch to live." (Ex. 22:18.)

Three hundred thousand persons were killed because of that text. The soil of our Republic has been stained with innocent blood because of that text. John Wesley said:

> "Giving up witchcraft is, in effect, *giving* up the Bible."

I ask my opponent if he believes in witches and whether they should be put to death.

We have a question put to Gladman. A woman writes:

> "I am a Sunday School teacher. How shall I explain 'concubine' to my pupils without giving them the impression that the Bible Patriarchs had more than one wife each?"

The Doctor replies:

> "Tell them 'concubine' is the Hebrew equivalent for stenographer."

The Patriarchs were polygamists.

There is a good deal of the Bible that is not pure literature. This is a mixed company. Read chapters 19 and 38 of the Book of Genesis, and ask yourself what would happen to a man if he wrote a book today and incorporated into it that kind of material. He would land behind prison bars.

Liberty of thought is alien to the Bible. A man must slay his wife, friend or daughter for religion. Duet. 13: 6-10. The Bible upholds tyranny. Rom. 13:1:

> "The powers that be are ordained of God. They that resist shall receive damnation."

If that be true, Thomas Jefferson, George Washington, Voltaire, and Thomas Paine are in hell, because they resisted the powers of their day. See also 1 Pet. 2: 13-14.

I will read what Moses ordered, and he said he got the order from God. He directs that innocent women and children be killed and commanded his officers: "—all the women and children who have not known man by lying with them, keep alive for yourselves." Numbers 31: 17 and 18.

Do you know how David got his first wife? He bought her with two hundred foreskins. 1 Sam. 18:27.

Just a word about the character of Christ. I quote you some of the teachings of Jesus.

"He that believeth not shall be damned." Mark 16:16.

What do you think of damnation for disbelief? Can a man believe contrary to the evidence? If you do not follow evidence as it appears to you, in the light of your experience, then you are a hypocrite. If the evidence convinces me that the Bible is false, where am I in error for disbelieving it? I would be a liar if I professed to believe it.

Mark, 9:45:

"Cast into hell, into the fire that shall never be quenched."

Jesus taught the doctrine of eternal punishment in hell. What good will it do to punish a man forever? It could not do anybody any good. Only a vindictive being, such as Jefferson said Jehovah is, could torture persons eternally for disbelieving something that seems to them to be untrue.

One of the worst features of Christianity is the doctrine of free-will— the doctrine that somehow you have the power to do as you please, regardless of your heredity and environment; that when a man does wrong he could have avoided doing it, and therefore, must be punished. It is a childish conception. When a child stumps its toe against the chair it may kick the chair, thinking that the chair is responsible. The more enlightened persons have given up the idea of free-will and vindictive punishment. This does not mean that we should let criminals run at large. To protect society, it is necessary to lock them up. Man is what his heredity and environment make him. When a mad dog comes down the street and bites a person, you kill the animal, but you don't torture it. If you would, you have the character of the being who invented hell.

If materialistic mechanism were not true, if man were not a machine, there would be no rational basis for effort. It would not be worthwhile to teach your child to be honest. Even Fundamentalist preachers adopt the mechanistic theory in winning souls; they use the emotional appeal that will bring the most converts.

When I last evening asked the question, whether or not God made certain disease germs, the Rev. Oliphant told you that disease germs were sent by God as a punishment for sin. Let me tell you something.

You take the class of people who make prostitution their profession. Do you think they are atheists? So far as I know we do not have a single prostitute in the United States as a member of our organization. Most of them are religious.

If it be true, as my opponent contends, that these venereal diseases are sent as a punishment for sin, is it not a most cruel method of punishing sin? The innocent often suffer as much as the guilty. Could not an omnipotent God find another punishment for sin than have babies born blind and women crippled for life?

The doctrine of faith makes the clergy a menace to civilization. It depreciates reason. We live in a dark forest with only a candle (reason) to guide us; and here comes a person, the priest, who says:

> "Blow it out and you will see better."

Faith is strongest among children and illiterate persons. If you will read, "The Belief in God and Immortality" by Professor Leuba you will find the most educated persons believe the least in the Bible. Of the psychologists eight percent believe in immortality, six percent of the women and two percent of the men. Women are in the majority in the churches. In the American Association for the Advancement of Atheism we have almost ten men to one woman. I will not say what the implications are, but man's brain is considerably larger than woman's.

In the remaining few minutes I shall quote from this word of God concerning the use of reason. This is from St. Paul:

> "Beware lest any man spoil you by philosophy and vain deceit."

Again:

> "Has not God made foolish the wisdom of the world."

The whole scheme of redemption is foolishness to me. Because our parents and forefathers disobeyed God, he would not be on good terms with us until his son was nailed on a cross. That is not reasonable.

Faith means mental slavery. Are you going to be the subject of the one who first gets your ear? If you had grown up in that part of Asia where Mohammedanism prevails, you would have accepted that religion.

In the Royal Society of England it was debated whether the placing of a fish in a barrel of water would increase the weight of the barrel and its contents. There were those who said it would not. King Charles commanded: "Make trial." They put the fish in the water and the weight increased. That is the way of science. Science is born of experience; religion is made of deductions from assertions.

In conclusion, let me *say* a word about the character of the clergy. I am not personal in this, but speak of them as a group. I have intimated to you they are no more moral than other persons, and in certain crimes are in the lead. They are not a very useful class of citizens. They pay half fare on the railroads; west of the Mississippi, they pay one-third. They are exempt from military duty. They do not pay taxes on their homes. What is their profession? You know what they are doing. They are selling you homes in heaven. It is the greatest swindle ever put over on the human race. Suppose that when a man offered to sell you a piece of land and you asked where it is and he replied: "I don't know;" "What direction?" "I don't know."

The clergy don't know where heaven is. They have not the slightest idea in which direction it lies, or how far distant. It is a gold brick, they ask you to live on hay, and promise pie in the sky when you die.

Oliphant's First Reply

Brother Chairman, Ladies and Gentlemen, Respected Opponent:

Contrary to the precedent set by Mr. Smith while in the negative, I intend to consider his arguments. I shall begin with the last things he said, while they are fresh in your minds.

He makes a number of statements which are not true. Preachers do not ride the trains on one-third fare. It is true that the railroad companies give ministers reduced rates; we pay two-thirds fare. Why do the railroads extend this courtesy? Being familiar with the development of this country, they know that the preachers have had a large part in building its civilization. They know that without the civilizing influence of the Christian religion they could not safely carry on their business. It is very largely due to the work of Christian missionaries that the railroad companies can now run their trains in every section of the United States, without having them attacked by Indian bands. In recognition of this service, and as an expression of gratitude for it, the railroad companies voluntarily extend the courtesy of a reduced rate to the ministry.

I know of no State in which homes owned by ministers are exempt from taxation. In some States property owned by churches, and used for religious services, is exempt. (Here Mr. Smith asked: "Most preachers live in parsonages, do they not?") Mr. Oliphant: I think not; I am of the opinion that the majority own their homes, or rent them. Where a house is furnished the minister, this is usually considered in determining his salary. The government exempts certain church property from taxation in recognition of a service considered more valuable than money.

Why are preachers exempt from military service? Because the government officials understand that there is a more vital work for ministers than carrying guns. I challenge Mr. Smith to name any class of men who rendered more service than the preachers during the World War.

It is charged that faith is contrary to reason. The *basis* for this charge is my friend's misunderstanding of faith. Faith is based on testimony—evidence. It "comes by hearing," and is "the evidence of things not seen." There can be no faith in the absence of evidence; and the evidence must be reasoned upon, and accepted intelligently. The Scriptures quoted to prove that Paul condemned the use of reason do not prove it. Paul condemned *a* philosophy that produced "vain deceit." He also condemned "science falsely so-called." (1 Tim. 6:20.) True science was never condemned by any Bible writer.

The apostle whom Mr. Smith charges with condemning reason, said:

"Prove all things; hold fast that which is good." (1 Thes. 5:21.)

Can atheists give us a better rule for determining truth? Do you know of a better way to use reasoning power?

All the atheist knows about historical characters is what he learns from testimony. I ask Mr. Smith if he believes Alexander the Great lived. If so, he exercises faith. He who rejects faith must reject all history.

The inference about the intelligence of women is amusing. I need not defend women. As someone has said, "She speaks for herself." Some of the most intellectual feats of the age have been accomplished by women. Mr. Smith's attitude toward woman is just another of the fruits of atheism. In spite of his boast of superior intelligence, I can name a number of women who would have no difficulty in meeting the arguments he has made in this debate.

We are told that there are more women than men in the churches; and more men than women in the atheist society. Since this is a discussion of morality, I ask what this fact implies. Does it indicate that atheism is more moral than Christianity? I challenge my opponent to say that women are more immoral than men.

The argument used to prove that man is a machine proves the reverse. Mr. Smith asks: "If man is not a machine—but has free-will, why teach your child to be honest?" Why sir, that is the very reason. Why do we not attempt to teach automobiles? Because they are machines. Machines can only operate according to the design of their maker; they do not think or reason. Human beings think, and therefore, should be taught to think correctly.

Mr. Smith contends that criminals 'cannot help committing crime; that they are criminal by nature. Being mere machines, the entire course of their lives is mapped out by heredity. Hence they should not be blamed for their crimes.' This is proved to be untrue by the thousands of criminals who have reformed. Many men who in the past have committed crimes are now respectable, law-abiding citizens. If man is a machine, there is no opportunity for reform, or for improvement of character.

What a hopeless doctrine atheism offers! Not only is a man a mere machine; but there is no one operating the machinery. If there is no God, we are machines running wild! Man has no responsibility. And then it is affirmed that this theory is conducive to morality! Will it make man better to remove all responsibility from him?

Machines do not grow; man grows. Machines do not procreate; man has the power to reproduce his species. To eliminate God, atheists must do more than show that man is a machine; they must prove that machines have the power to create themselves.

The Bible is charged with teaching unquestioned obedience to governments. It is true that Christians are taught to respect in the proper manner duly constituted authority. Christians are good citizens, respecting and supporting their government. But should unrighteous authorities make laws which conflict with the law of God; if decision must be made between God and human government, the Bible says:

"We ought to obey God rather than men." 5:29.

That the early Christians were governed by this rule is evidenced by the fact that when human authority forbade the preaching of the gospel, they continued to preach it. Atheism breeds anarchy. If the authority of God is rejected, what authority can be accepted?

Mr. Smith charges that Jesus condemns men for not believing, when no evidence is given. The evidence for Christianity is overwhelming. A vast majority of those who have heard it accept it. Jesus also says:

"If any man will do his will, he shall know the teaching, whether it be of God." (Jno. 7:17.)

Any man who honestly wants to know the truth and to practice it, can learn the truth. I am convinced that the big reason for disbelief is not a lack of evidence, but an unwillingness to live right.

My opponent brings the old charge that the Bible contains impure statements; literature that should not be read before a mixed audience. Text books used in medical colleges contain passages which it might not be wise to read before a mixed assembly. I have seen pictures in medical journals which I would not enjoy exhibiting to an audience of ladies. But the doctors must have these books; they are indispensible to the teaching of anatomy. We do not condemn these books because of these things. They were not written for indiscriminate public reading. The Bible deals with man's spiritual anatomy. Sin is a disease; the Bible offers a remedy. Some sins are so vile that we would not want to discuss them in a mixed assembly. Still, these hideous sins are committed by mankind; and, therefore, must be dealt with. To point out the remedy, the Bible must first describe the disease. The mention in the Bible of an unclean thing is always to condemn it.

Bob Ingersoll charged that the Bible mentions the most vile things "without the least bit of humor." Ingersoll unconsciously confessed the reason for this charge against the Bible. If the Bible made a joke of immorality, infidels would like it. But, because the Bible deals seriously with the vile pollutions of ungodly men, infidels criticize it. It is the "hit dog that howls."

It is charged that eternal punishment is immoral. We have sympathy for the man who is being punished by the State. I do not like to see men go to the penitentiary. But who is to blame for the punishment of criminals? Not the State, but the criminals themselves. So it is with God's punishment of the wicked. God cannot be blamed.

I may not be able to see the justice of eternal punishment. My view of life is too limited for me to attempt to judge matters of eternity. If I were asked to describe a plant and tell its uses, having never seen more than a tiny portion of its leaf, I should not be able to do so. While, after I have examined the whole plant, I can describe it, and perhaps explain the purpose of its existence, I see but a small arc broken from the great circle of eternity. Hence I cannot explain the things of eternity.

The child often thinks the punishment administered by his parents is unjust and unreasonable. In later years he understands the reason for it. We are but children in regard to eternity; we must leave its government in the hands of a loving Heavenly Father, knowing that "He doeth all things well."

Mr. Smith says atheists have built schools and hospitals. I have asked him to name one. So far, he has not done so. My friends, he has a good reason for not naming a school or hospital that atheists have built. There is no such institution in the world.

In explaining this situation, my opponent say that there were no avowed atheists before his "4A Society" was organized. Why my friends, some of you remember that Stanley J. Clark (who was in the audience last night) debated these very issues with Joe S. Warlick in this town some twelve of fifteen years ago. (Here Mr. Smith asked: "But did he call himself an atheist?") Mr. Oliphant: I'll put that question back to you—did he? (Mr. Smith: "He did not.") Mr. Oliphant: Mr. Clark affirmed the very same things you are affirming. Why did he not call himself an atheist? (Mr. Smith: "Bigoted Christians made it too unpopular.") Mr. Oliphant: Then you admit that Clark was an atheist, but charge that he was too cowardly to admit it. I would not charge Stanley Clark with cowardice. I believe he was an atheist, and attempted to defend his atheism. I am more charitable toward him than you are. Everybody understood at the time of that debate that Mr. Clark was an atheist.

Mr. Smith is trying to give undue prestige to the organization of which he is president. There have been atheists for centuries. But I do not care to quibble about names: let Mr. Smith name an educational institution or a hospital that was built by anti-religionists—I don't care what name they wore. Sir, can you name such an institution that was founded by those opposed to religion?

He says no Bible-believing Christian ever built a hospital. Investigate the history of the hospitals of our nation, and see who is responsible for their existence. Mr. Smith quotes:

> "Is any sick among you? let him call for the elders of the church; and let them pray over him anointing him with oil in the name of the Lord."

Olive oil was one of the most commonly used medicines of that day. It seems to me that in modern language, James says: "Pray for the sick, and use the best known remedies in nature." God has given man intelligence. He should use his intelligence in combating disease, and at the same time, pray to God.

When Mr. Smith charges that Christianity forbids the use of a physician he speaks without knowledge. Jesus said:

> "They that are whole need not a physician; but they that are sick." (Lu. 5:31.)

Luke, the disciple who recorded this statement, was a physician. Mr. Smith's charge is contrary to the facts. He should inform himself on the teaching of the Bible before he attempts to say what it teaches.

I stated in the beginning of the debate that I would not attempt to defend perversions of Christianity. All of my friend's talk about Christians closing the schools of Athens, and being responsible for the Dark Ages, is irrelevant. Everyone who has studied the history of medieval times knows that the institution then posing as the church was far from being like the church established by our Lord. Christianity should not be condemned because of the conduct of those who have apostatized from it.

Even this corruption of Christianity is a vindication of the inspiration of the New Testament; it was foretold. (See II Thes. 2:3; Acts 20:30; I

Tim. 4: 1-3.)

The crimes of the Dark Ages were the fruits of Christianity's being rejected, rather than practiced. The teachings of Jesus Christ and His apostles could never bring about such conditions. Christianity must be judged by the teachings of its Author.

The charge is again made that educated people do not believe in God. I refuted that charge yesterday by the statements of a number of the most scholarly men in America. Mr. Smith now refers to Dr. Leuba's book. I have examined this book. Dr. Leuba's findings are not what they might appear to be. His investigation was not conducted fairly. He did not ask the scientists to whom he addressed his questionnaire if they believed in God; but prepared his own question to which they were to answer yes or no. Some questions cannot be answered so simply. If I were to ask Mr. Smith if he has quit stealing, he would not want to answer with a simple yes or no.

Dr. Leuba's question embraced a belief in the answer to prayer, and intimated a specific method of answer. Many people believe wholeheartedly in an intelligent Creator, who is interested in His creatures; and at the same time they hesitate to say just to what degree, and in what way, He answers our prayers.

While Dr. Leuba's question was unfair, it is interesting to note that forty-one percent of the scientists answered in the affirmative. To me, this indicates that forty-one percent of the scientists who answered were so firm in their conviction that, lest their answers be used against God, they affirmed everything Dr. Leuba asked. No one can justly charge the other fifty-eight percent with unbelief, simply because they refused to accept the position Dr. Leuba tried to hand them.

Mr. Smith has seen a few newspaper accounts of preachers having committed crime, and he jumps at the conclusion that preachers are more immoral than others. It is true that some, preachers are sinners; but their sin is not caused by Christianity. When they sin they go contrary to the gospel they preach. But Mr. Smith has an exaggerated estimate of the number of this kind of preacher. I once criticized the editor of a great daily paper for "displaying" the accounts of preachers' crimes. He said

"Do you know why we print the, story of a preacher's immorality on the front page? Because it is news. We do not display articles about the good done by preachers, because that is not news. Everybody knows that. It is his mistakes that are unusual—hence, news. We do not write front-page stories about the misdemeanors of great criminals. You should consider every newspaper story about a preacher's immorality a compliment to the ministry."

The atheist tract, "Religion and Roguery," does not prove that religion causes crime. The statistics given do not indicate the number of irreligious in the penal institutions. All who expressed a church preference are listed as religious. This is not necessarily true. Even an atheist may prefer one church above another. Such dastard crimes as that committed by the two young atheists, Leopold and Loeb, are but logical fruits of the atheistic philosophy of life.

I deny his statement that most college professors are atheists. He offers no proof; until he attempts to prove it, I shall simply say it is untrue.

Let me give you an example of the honesty of atheist scientists. Ernst Haeckel, an atheist, in an effort to prove that in certain rudimentary stages animals of wholly different species exactly resemble each other; printed pictures of what purported to be embryos of a man, an ape and a dog. He also printed pictures supposed to be the embryos of a dog, a fowl and a turtle—all being identical.

Soon Professor Ruthmeyer, of Basle, discovered that the embryos were in both instances, the same plate printed three different times. This was proved by accidental scratches on the face of the plates. This fact was brought to Haeckel's attention. He did not deny it.

In 1908 Haeckal published a defense to put to rest what he termed "brutal fuss" and "Christian slanders." In this reply he freely confesses that a small portion of his embryo illustration had been "faked," but this had been done "in connection with such picture when the available data was insufficient," and that he was compelled to fill in the "lacunal with hypotheses, and to construct the missing links by comparative synthesis." Quite an alibi for outright dishonesty! When scientists try to prove atheism, they sometimes do peculiar things!

Dr. Horace J. Bridges was a member of the Rationalist Press Association, which association issued Haeckel's "Riddles of the Universe," and "Evolution of Man." Dr. Bridges calls Haeckel's essay on "Science and Christianity" a "farrago of ignorant nonsense." He then tells how Professor Freidrich Loofs of Halle, Germany, denounced Haeckel, deliberately choosing such language as would make it possible for Haeckel to prosecute him for libel. Dr. Bridges points out that Haeckel did not see fit to do so. He also says that the controversy disclosed the fact that Haeckel had gotten his information from a "tenth-rate free-thought book by an obscure English journalist." Dr. Bridges remarks that "no such crushing exposure of presumptuous ignorance was ever made before in the case of a man of academic training and career." (Criticisms of Life, pgs. 77-120.)

Mr. Smith talks a great deal about reason. Reason has been the god of many infidels. When man succeeds in getting God out of his mind, he usually resorts to some form of idolatry. Robert Ingersoll said:

> "We are looking for the time when the useful shall be the honorable; and when Reason, throned upon the world's brain, shall be King of Kings, and God of Gods." (The Gods, pg. 64.)

Let us notice France during her Revolutionary period. We have here a most clear-cut example of the results of atheism. Dr. Shailer Matthews, Professor in the University of Chicago, speaking of Denis Diderot, D'Alembert, Helvetius, Holbach, Rosseau, and others, says:

> "They attacked not only Christianity, but immortality and God as well."

As for morals, the historian tells us that they would have "none of, such conventions as marriage, and championed the most extreme of free-love doctrines." He says that they found in "the natural, or uncivilized man the ideal being."

Rosseau lived some ten or twelve years with a woman of "accommodating morals," left her, because of a rival lover, when he was thirty years old. He then went to Paris, where he lived with an illiterate maid-servant, Therese Levasseur, by whom he had five children, each of whom he promptly sent to the foundling asylum.

Rosseau contended that the progress of the arts and sciences had tended to corrupt morals; that civilization was a curse, and the uncivilized man the ideal of life. The historian points out that "the millennium of his gospel was The Reign of Terror." (The French Revolution, pgs, 63-66.)

After the overthrow of the French Monarchy, by the masses, led by the atheistic leaders, the "Convention of Public Safety" had full sway. Dr. Matthews says their "actions were coarse and irrational."

> "On November 10, 1793, the convention established the worship of Reason. Decked out in red liberty caps, the deputies went in a body to the cathedral of Notre Dame, and consecrated it to the Goddess of Reason, whose representative, a beautiful actress, sat on the altar, while women of the town danced in the darmagnole in the nave."

The historian says the service then degenerated into a "shameless orgy."

In Paris, the words: "Liberty and Equality," were inscribed over the door of every householder; yet the Committee of Public Safety suppressed freedom of thought, opened letters, instituted a secret police, destroyed right of trial by jury, and put hundreds of poor lace women to death because they wanted to begin their work with prayer.

The City of Lyons, which had offered resistance to their armies, was ordered annihilated, and the name of its site changed. Some two thousand persons were massacred during five months.

An order of a levy en masse started a rebellion of the people in La Vendee (lying on the Bay of Biscay, between the Loire and La Rochelle). After they were defeated, the Committee of Public Safety undertook to punish them. Troops were sent, villages were burned, thousands of people were executed. At least eighteen hundred people were shot without trial. This method, however, proved too slow for these blood-thirsty atheists. They turned to drowning. Men and women were stripped naked, bound and sent out by companies in old vessels which were sunk in the Loire. Perhaps two thousand were killed this way within less than two months. This terrible program continued until the mouth of the river was stopped with corpses, and thousands of people died from pestilence resulting from unburied bodies. (French Revolution, *pgs.* 245, 246.)

All this, ladies and gentleman, is but a part of the picture of a country ruled by atheism. Is this the atheist's conception of morality? May God keep us far from such!

I charge that the philosophy of atheism is brutal, savage and immoral.

In Mr. Smith's tract, "Godless Evolution," he quotes Cardinal Manning as saying: "Darwinism is a brutal philosophy—to-wit, there is no God, and an ape is our Adam." Mr. Smith follows this quotation with one word of his own: "Correct." In other words, Mr. Smith accepts Darwinism as his philosophy, and then admits that it is "brutal." I need no further proof of my first charge. I have Mr. Smith's own words in substantiation of it.

I quote again from this tract, Mr. Smith's words:

> "The crowning glory of evolution is to have shown how to improve the human stock—not by prayers to God; no, not even by education, but by selective breeding. Evolution links man with the animals. The laws of heredity operate as inexorably with him as with them. Mental and moral dualities are no exception, for these have a physical basis, which is inherited."

I want you to notice that Smith says education has no, part in the development of the human race. He is the man who has been charging that Christianity is opposed to education! Ile also says, "Mental and moral qualities are no exception." These too, must be disregarded in his brutish program. To continue the quotation:

> " 'To grade up the cattle of the country,' a rich religious stockman demands: 'A pure-bred bull for every herd.' There is but one way to grade up the human race —to let only the best breed. This does not mean that the State should adopt the primary principle of animal breeding, so that the best male in a community should be the father of its children? But if it were not immoral, the principle would be the greatest possible engine for elevating the human race, compared to which other means are feeble."

There you have it, in Mr. Smith's own words: Place human life on the same plane with that of the brute, disregard all mentality and morality; simply develop the biggest brute possible! This is the "morality" of atheism.

Smith says that "if it were not immoral, the best male in a community should be the father of the children." But, who told him it would be immoral? According to the standard of atheism, it would not be immoral. Sir, the only reason you do not attempt the practice of your heathenish, degrading plan of "breeding" is that you live in a country whose government has too many Christian standards to permit it! Why don't you go to some heathen country, where God's old Bible has never gone? You should fit in nicely with the lowest grade of heathenism. Perhaps some strong "physically-developed" cannibal would eat you. At least, you could there try on human beings your brute system of living. I am of the opinion that such an opportunity will never be given you in a civilized country.

I want to continue the quotation from Mr. Smith's "Godless Evolution:"

> "Weakness of mind and body are now transmitted to increasing numbers in each generation, when, Nature, left alone, would weed them out. Birth control would lessen the evil."

No wonder atheists have never established hospitals! Mr. Smith advocates letting "nature weed out" the weak. In other words, do not take care of the weak or the sick; just let them die! I am wondering if that principle would have rid the world of my opponent! Perhaps not, since mentality and morality are not to be considered. He would possibly survive on the basis of a strictly beast "survival of the fittest."

My friends, can you imagine a more beastly philosophy? This principle—of letting nature "weed out" the physically weak, would have deprived the world of some of the greatest characters that have ever lived. Many of the greatest minds have been in weak bodies. John T. Faris wrote a book, "Men Who Made Good," in which he gives sketches of the lives of twenty-six men—artists, authors and lecturers, editors and publishers, inventors, philanthropists, religious workers, scientists, statesmen. Nearly all of these men had a handicap of heredity or environment. Without the aid and protection of Christian society, these men might have been "weeded out" by nature. The world would have been loser.

My charge that atheism is brutal, savage and immoral, has been proved. Let my opponent attempt to refute it.

One of the "fundamentals of atheism," as expressed by Mr. Smith is "that happiness here and now should be the motive of conduct." If it gives me happiness "here and now" to, knock a man in the head and rob him, what prevents my doing so? Atheism makes no difference between a man and a beast. If it is not wrong to kill a hog, why is it wrong to kill a man?

I challenge my opponent to show any reason why he should not be killed. If a mad dog goes about endangering the physical health of people, we kill him. Mr. Smith goes over the country trying to rob people of their spiritual health and happiness; why shouldn't he be killed, like the mad dog? Rejecting God and the Bible as he does, he cannot offer a single reason why it would be wrong for someone to shoot him. Again I ask him: Why is it more wrong to kill a man than to kill a snake?

Atheism, if adopted by a nation, would lead to the most chaotic condition imaginable; no man respecting the rights of any other; every man "a law unto himself," looking only to his own happiness "here and now." The French Revolution is but a small sample.

I again ask Mr. Smith to show us atheism's standard of morality. And again, I charge that it has none. To be an atheist, you need not believe anything; you need not do anything, you need not be anything.

As to religion and crime, let me give you a few statements from men who should know. Judge Fawcett of New York City has said:

> "In the five years I have been sitting on the bench, I have had 2,700 boys before me for sentence and not one of them was an attendant at Sunday School."

Judge John R. Newcomber, of the Municipal Court of Chicago, reported that as prosecuting attorney and presiding judge, he had handled more than one hundred thousand cases. Out of this vast number of cases, not as many as ten defendants were boys or girls who had been regular attendants in the Protestant Sunday Schools up to the time of their majority. (Week Day Religious Instruction, introduced by John H. Finley, LL.D., Associate Editor, New York Times, formerly Commissioner of Education, New York State.)

The work of Judge Hoyt as Judge of the Children's Court of New York City, led him to say:

> "If our experience in the Children's Court has proved one thing, it is that religion is essential in the training of children and that no lasting good can be achieved when their spiritual development is neglected." (Quicksands of Youth, pg. 229.)

Dr. Wm. H. Cox says:

> "In Chicago in the five years up to 1915, out of 55,000 persons below the age of sixteen who had passed through the hands of the police, fewer than one-sixth had ever heard of the Ten Commandments."

Judge B. J. Humphreys says that in his twenty years on the bench he cannot recall but one of the thousands of criminals brought before him who had had a Sunday School training. (Quoted by Charles S. Knight, "Both Sides of Evolution." pg. 160.)

We shall introduce one more witness on this point. These facts were reported in the Evangelical Messenger, July 7, 1929:

> "During the last twenty years 20,000 young men between the ages of eighteen and twenty-five years have been admitted to the Indiana Reformatory, now at Pendleton. More than 85 percent of these were from broken homes—fathers and mothers had separated and remarried. There was not a single Boy Scout in the number. Only four percent of the twenty thousand belonged to a church."

These are facts, stated by men who have been in a position to see the effects of religious training on young lives. I put these plain statements up in contrast to Smith's garbled statistics.

I want you people to remember that, though Mr. Smith is supposed to be affirming that atheism is conducive to good morals, he has not said one word in defense of the morality of atheism. He has done nothing but attack Christianity. This method of debating is in harmony with the whole program of atheism; it is entirely destructive.

In the few minutes I have left, I shall introduce a few of the principles of morality taught in the New Testament.

The religion of Jesus Christ teaches: Avoiding hatred (Mt. 5:21,22); No lustful thinking (Mt. 5:24); No unfair judgments (Mt. 7:1,2); Love of enemies. (Mt. 5:44); Reconciliation (Mt. 5:24); Non-resistence (Mt. 5:38,39); Avoiding Anxiety (Mt. 6:25-29); Self-examination (Mt. 7:3-5); Respect for government. (Rom. 13:1-7); Equality of man (Jas. 2:1-4); A universal Brotherhood (Mt. 23:9); Forgiveness (Mt. 11:25); Thrift and industry (Eph. 4:28); Progress (Heb. 6:1); The value of truth (2 Cor. 13:8); Truth as the basis for freedom (Jno. 8:32); Humility (Lk. 14:11); Benevolence (Acts, 20:35); Honesty (Rom. 12:17); Single standard of morals (Gal. 3:28); Unselfishness (Rom. 12:10).

Consider the Golden Rule:

> "Therefore all things whatsoever ye would that men should do to you, do ye even so to them; for this is the law and the prophets." (Mt. 7:12.)

This expresses the world's only perfect standard of conduct. I challenge any atheist to find a single fault in it.

I could continue indefinitely in naming the principles of righteousness given in God's word. I do not deem it necessary. To reduce this question to the most definite, concise issue, I am willing to risk the whole proposition on this challenge: I challenge Mr. Smith to name any principle of morality that I cannot read in the Bible. Let him mention any virtue he may think of, and I will read it in this Book—the Christian's standard of life.

Smith's Second Affirmative

Mr. Chairman, Ladies and Gentlemen, Honored Opponent:

I have been asked to name one moral principle my opponent cannot find in the Bible. Perhaps I cannot; you can prove most anything by the Bible. It contains contradictory teachings on most every subject. But the good teachings were not original with Jesus or with the authors of the Bible. They stole them—or took them—from earlier writers. The Golden Rule was taught by various philosophers long before Jesus came into the world.

My opponent seems to take special pleasure in accusing me of egotism because I deny the existence of God. I do not care to make any personal remarks of the character he has made against me. But if it be egotism to deny the existence of one god, where is the humility in saying that there is only one god? Why is it more egotistical to deny the existence of God than to deny the existence of hobgoblins, and demons?

It is not necessary to deny the existence of God to be an atheist. The man who has no god is an atheist, though he may not have the courage to admit the fact. I can think of no more egotistical person that he who believes that a being who created the innumerable myriads of stars and directs the universe is interested in him.

It is charged that atheism is anarchistic. The charge is baseless. We accept the government. We believe in the United States Constitution. We are a duly chartered organization. I will tell you who are the law-breakers in this country. You have no more law-breaking class than the clergy, who are willing to disregard the Constitution in the separation of Church and State. They want to get into the State, and bootleg their religion into our public schools. Some of them, as chaplains, are in the army and navy, paid for, in part, by the atheist. That nothing so deadens the moral conscience as religion was shown by the persecution of me last year in Arkansas. It was stated last night that I was arrested there because of my blasphemous remarks. What is the status of the Arkansas case? The bigoted Christians in Arkansas arrested me, though I was violating no law. I was distributing atheist tracts when I was arrested on a charge of blasphemy. By their actions, my prosecutors have exonerated me. They dismissed one case and have refused to set the other for trial. They know they had no right to arrest me.

In Arkansas today, an atheist cannot testify in court, not even in his own defense. A Christian can steal an atheist's watch and the atheist cannot testify against him. A Christian can shoot down an atheist in cold blood, and if only atheists are witnesses, the Christian will go free. That is the law which the bigoted Christians in Arkansas do not want tested. Amendment 14 of the United States Constitution says that no State shall deny a citizen of the United States the equal protection of the laws. They are violating the Federal Constitution. No wonder they don't want to stay in court.

You heard it charged that Ernst Haeckel, a German scientist, was guilty of fraud. That is too long a subject for me to go into in this rebuttal. I challenge my opponent to deny that scientists have vindicated him. The facts are set forth in "Haeckel's Answer to the Jesuits."

You have heard a great deal about the French Revolution, painted in the colors of eloquence of which my opponent is capable. The number of persons killed in that revolution is insignificant compared to those killed in obedience to certain Bible commands. Witchcraft and slavery are thorns in the flesh of Christians. You have observed that my opponent has not replied to this except by saying that God regulated slavery. A God capable of making the world and the stars would be able to stop slavery. He could have said: "Thou shalt not have slaves." Was there not room on those stones Moses got on Sinai to write another command? The Bible deity gave instructions how to brand a slave, by piercing through the ear. Ex. 21:6.

The Rev. Oliphant has not said a word about witchcraft. I ask him to tell you whether or not he believes in witches. If there be a true God there should be true witches. In Pennsylvania last year they put three boys in the penitentiary for following the command given by Jehovah not to suffer witches to live.

My opponent did not refute the statement that the French Revolutionists were first to abolish slavery. He did not say anything about Alexander Campbell, who said that according to the Bible slavery is not immoral. I ask you, did Campbell tell the truth or not? He is the founder of the Christian Church. He said:

"According to the Bible, slavery is not immoral."

I say Campbell is right, but that his Bible is wrong.

What is morality? What is the original meaning of the word? It comes from the Latin word "Mor," plural, "mores," meaning "custom." Morals are good customs.

You remember those vivid pictures which our oratorical friend painted of the French Revolution. He has made a mountain out of a molehill. The French Revolution at the worst is a dim copy of what the Christians did before that; and what they did was a dimmer copy of what God did in establishing a hell where they torture persons who do not believe, torture them for not being hypocrites. What in the French Revolution is comparable to that? When they were persecuting those poor heretics for not believing the stories told in the Bible, they made them suffer as much as possible. Servetus was burned because he did not believe in infant damnation and because he said the Holy land was not fertile. The Bible says it was a land "flowing with milk and honey." Every sensible man knows it is a barren country, and has always been so. How did they burn him? They used green wood so as to have a slow fire to prolong the agony. As the victim was burning, he asked: "Did not the watch and the gold chain that you took from me suffice to buy enough dry wood?" The inquisition is man's nearest approach to God's hell. No atheist would be guilty of creating such a place as hell. I ask my opponent, "If the devil were to die, would God create another?"

"Atheists have no standard of morals," say the clergy. The charge is untrue. Happiness here and now determines our conduct. The Golden Rule expresses enlightened self-interest. It was taught by pagan philosophers long before Jesus was invented. Conscience is not the voice of God, but is the result of social experience. Morals have not been revealed, but have evolved. The Bible is not a safe moral guide, for it sanctions slavery, witchcraft persecution, intolerance of opinion, subjection of women, damnation for disbelief, and many other immoralities. The history of the Christian Church and the record of Christians today refute the assertions of my opponent.

Reference has been made to Rosseau. He was not an atheist. It seems Rev. Oliphant is unable to distinguish between an atheist and an infidel. Leopold and Loeb are offered as examples of what atheism leads to. What about Hickman, Hight, and Hotelling, a few of the religionists who in recent times have committed dastardly deeds?

Now we come to the question of eugenics. The Rev. Oliphant takes exception to my statement that only the best should breed. What are you going to do? Let the inferior breed? If you do, you are going to get hillbillies and morons. A weak-minded person is apt to produce weak-minded offspring. According to Christians, every person has a soul. They try to save every defective person that comes into the world. They let the deaf and dumb multiply. In a few States, the leaders are beginning to take some thought of tomorrow. They don't want to debase the stock of the human race. They are passing more laws for the sterilization of the unfit. Christians oppose that, and also oppose birth control.

I conclude with an account of a recent occurrence in Newark, New Jersey. A family there had as many children as the parents were able to provide for. The mother was in delicate health and did not want to bear more children. They were Catholics, but the mother went to the birth control clinic and obtained information on how to prevent conception. The husband found out what she was doing and called in the priest, who said she was committing a mortal sin against God. What could the poor woman do? She threw away her medicines and appliances, but declared that if ever her husband forced his relations upon her she would not bear children—she would commit suicide first. The husband did force relations upon her, and the next night on returning from work he found the house had burned down, with his wife and children inside. It was published in the newspapers that the cause of the tragedy was unknown. That is what Christianity causes—unhappiness in this world. Atheism teaches that happiness here and now should be the motive of conduct.

Oliphant's Second Reply

Brother Chairman, Ladies and Gentlemen, Respected Opponent:

I am now to make the last speech on the present proposition. I do not have much to do as I am following my opponent and, consequently, when he makes no argument I have nothing to answer.

I thank the gentleman for his admission that he cannot name a moral principle not contained in the Bible. I want it to go on record that the president of the American Association for the Advancement of Atheism has admitted publicly that the Bible contains a complete system of morals—at least, that he cannot think of anything that is lacking.

Mr. Smith says the Golden Rule was taught before the time of Christ. His only proof is his assertion. Sir, your word is not authority with this or any other intelligent audience. If, as Mr. Smith says, preachers do not have to prove what they say; is it not a pity that he is not a preacher?

With reference to my charge that for one to say he KNOWS there is no God is egotism, my friend asks why it is more egotistical to deny all gods than to deny one. The proof that the religions of many gods (polytheism) are degenerate forms of the original religion of one God (monotheism), still stands. I offered it in my first speech; my opponent has never noticed it.

I am charged with egotism because of my believing that God will hear my prayers. If that be egotism, it is in behalf of the race of men—not an exaltation of myself. Nor, do I contend that men are worthy of the attention of God; but because man is a rational being, capable of development, God has seen fit to be "mindful of him." We thank God that this is true.

Mr. Smith is certainly inconsistent in his definitions of an atheist. When he is trying to dodge a charge made against atheists, he minimizes the number, and makes a clear distinction between "infidels" and "atheists." When he wants to attribute something good to atheism, he makes every man who is not devoutly religious, an atheist. There are many people not actively engaged in church work who will earnestly contend for the existence and goodness of God.

The most foolish absurdity that I have heard is Mr. Smith's statement (made last night) that he could come into this pulpit and say just the reverse of what was said last Sunday, and it would be accepted; provided he assumed a pious expression. No sane man believes that statement to be true. I would not make such an absurd assertion in regard to an atheist meeting. I could, with as much reason, say that I could preach the gospel to an atheist meeting, and that it would meet their approval; provided I assumed an "impious and blasphemous" look. The attitude of this audience toward his speeches indicates whether they accept his doctrines.

We are charged with being law-breakers in not adhering to the doctrine of separation of Church and State. I firmly believe in the separation of Church and State. Jesus taught that men should "render unto Caesar (civil governments) the things that are Caesar's, and unto God the things that are God's." (Mt. 22:21.) Nor, do we demand the teaching of religion in the Public Schools. We do insist that if religion is not to be taught, that anti-religion shall not be taught. Is it lawlessness to insist that the religion of an overwhelming majority of the tax-payers shall not be attacked in institutions supported by taxes?

I believe in freedom of speech, hence, would not want to see Mr.

Smith imprisoned for his teaching. I do not think he can do much harm among intelligent people. However, there is some justification for the State of Arkansas forbidding an atheist to testify in court. Testimony is offered "in the name of God." How can a man testify in the name of a God whom he does not think exists? No honest atheist would so testify.

My friend has a great deal to say about Alexander Campbell's attitude toward slavery. I am not obligated to defend Mr. Campbell's position. A man may be influenced by his environment. Campbell lived among a people who believed in slavery. I do not know that he ever gave the question much consideration. I have a high regard for Brother Campbell. I believe him to have been a great and good man, but, as a Christian, with no denominational obligations, I have as much right to differ from him as from any other teacher. I am not a member of a church founded by Alexander Campbell. Mr. Smith should inform himself or refrain from speaking on that subject.

My opponent denies that Ernst Haeckel was guilty of fraud. He does something for Mr. Haeckel that *he* refused to do for himself. Haeckel admitted that he "faked" the embryo pictures. Possibly some so-called scientists did vindicate him. Haeckel said "hundreds" of them were guilty of the same thing.

Mr. Smith says "morals" comes from the Latin "mores," meaning customs. It is easy to see that one's customs (practices) bear close relation to his morals (as we now use the word). Granting that "good morals" are "good customs," does not help the position of atheism. What are good customs? What standard of customs (morals) does atheism offer? How can any man determine from atheism what are good customs, or morals?

Mr. Smith implies that religion was responsible for the terrible crime of Edward Hickman. Just the reverse is true; lack of religion and the presence of atheism caused this heinous crime. Just before Hickman was hanged he handed a message to Warden Holohan, who asked a newspaper man to read it aloud. Among other things, the statement contained these words:

> "A young man who tries to build character without truth is like the house built on the sands. It is very dangerous for young

men to neglect their spiritual welfare. During high school I took an interest in evolution and atheism and denied Christian faith. Therefore, I became susceptible to worse errors and finally took up crime and murder." (Clipped from press reports, by Free Tract Society, Los Angeles, Cal.).

You see we have from Hickman, himself, the reason for his crime. No doubt Mr. Smith can find where crimes have been committed by religious people. False religion may have contributed to some crimes; but the religion of Jesus Christ never caused any one to commit a crime. On the contrary, it is the strongest deterrent of crime the world has ever known.

If any individual atheists are moral, their morality is stolen from Christianity; they are moral because of the influence of religion upon their lives.

Christianity does not cause unhappiness in this world, as Mr. Smith charges. The spirit of the Christian religion is one of rejoicing. (See Phil. 3:1; 4:4; 1 Pet. 1:8.) Christianity condemns those things that are not conducive to lasting happiness, and authorizes conduct that gives happiness "here and now," as well as eternal happiness.

It is only a misinterpreted Bible that produces unhappiness. What has caused more unhappiness than misunderstood science? Shall we condemn science because some have harmed themselves by a wrong application of its principles?

Christians did not kill Servetus. He was burned by fanatical apostates. Mr. Smith cannot consistently charge Christianity with such crimes, unless he can show that the Founder of Christianity sanctioned such deeds. This, he cannot do.

I do not believe in infant damnation any more than did Servetus. The Bible does not teach it; on the contrary, Jesus taught that children are fit subjects for the Kingdom of Heaven, (See Mt. 18:3; 19:14; Mk. 10:14.)

Our friend says every sensible man knows that Palestine is a barren country, and "has always been so." This is just another sample of his disregard for facts. That this land was at one time fertile and productive, a "land flowing with milk and honey," can be established by an abundance of authority outside of the Bible. Josephus, Jewish historian, says of the Galileans:

> "Their soil is universally rich and fruitful, and full of the plantations of trees of all sorts, insomuch that it invites the most slothful to take pains in its cultivation by its fruitfulness; accordingly, it is all cultivated by its inhabitants, and no part of it lies idle. Moreover, the cities lie here very thick, and the very many villages there are here are everywhere so full of people, by the richness of their soil, that the very least of them contained above fifteen thousand inhabitants." (Jewish Wars, book 3, Chapter 3.)

Tacitus, Roman historian, gives this testimony:

> "The soil is rich and fertile; besides the fruits known in Italy, the palm and balm trees flourish in great luxuriance." (History, book 6, section 6.)

Edward Gibbon, in his "Decline and Fall of the Roman Empire," says:

> "From the age of David to that of Heraclius the country was overspread with ancient and flourishing cities." (Chapter 51.)

It is true that the country is now desolate. This condition was foretold by Old Testament writers. (See Lev. 26:22;31-34; Deut. 29:22-25.) Its desolation is a most minute fulfillment of these Old Testament prophecies.

That Palestine was not always desolate, can be proved by infidel writers. C. M. F. Volney, comparing the present with the ancient condition of the country, says:

> "We are informed by the philosophical geographer, Strabo, that the territories of Jamnia and Joppa in Palestine, alone were formerly so populous as to be able to bring forty thousand armed mien into the field. At present they could scarcely furnish three thousand. From the accounts we have of Judea in the time of Titus, and which are to be esteemed tolerably accurate, that country must have contained four millions of inhabitants; but at present there are not perhaps above three

thousand * * There is nothing in nature or experience to contradict the great population of high antiquity; without appealing to the positive testimony of history, there are innumerable monuments that depose in favor of the fact." (Travels through *Syria* and Egypt.-1783-4-5, ch. 32.)

The same infidel writer also says:

> "The plain country is rich and light, calculated for the greatest fertility." (Travels, ch. 1, sec. 6.)

Because infidels do not want to admit the fulfillment of Moses' prophecies, they assert that Palestine never flourished as the Bible says it did. But, unfortunately for their cause, they are refuted by reliable historians, as well as by their own writers. He who is familiar with history cannot fail to see in this country as it stands today, conclusive proof of the inspiration of the Old Testament writers.

Mr. Smith asks: "If the devil were to die, would God create another?" I think not, there are enough atheists in hell to fully replace him. I realize there is no sense in this answer; neither is there any in his question. I am forced to the advice of Solomon: "Answer a fool according to his folly."

Thomas Jefferson is brought up again. Not only was Jefferson not an atheist; he was not an infidel, in any sense that will help my opponent. In addition to the quotations from Jefferson I gave you last night, I Want you to hear him again:

> "To the corruptions of Christianity I am indeed opposed; but not to the genuine precepts of Jesus himself." (Letter to Benjamin Rush, 1803, F. VIII, 223.)

Referring to his "Philosophy of Jesus," Jefferson says:

> "It is a document in proof that I am a REAL CHRISTIAN, that is to say, a disciple of the doctrines of Jesus, very different from the Platonists, who call ME infidel and THEMSELVES Christians and preachers of the Gospel, while they draw all their characteristic dogmas from what its author never said nor *saw.*" (Letter to Charles Thompson.)

In a letter to his daughter, written In 1803, Mr. Jefferson characterized the charge that be was irreligious as "the libels published against me."

Do these statements sound like Jefferson belonged in the, camp occupied by Smith? The faith of Jefferson cannot possibly be reduced to less than that of Unitarianism. The fact that he said, "I am a Materialist," proves nothing. There is now a religious sect known as Materialists. It depends altogether on how you use the term.

Mr. Jefferson certainly did not agree with Mr. Smith on the morality of Christianity. In a letter to Wm. Canby, 1813, he says:

> "Of all the systems of morality, ancient and modern, which have come under my observation, none appear to me so pure as that of Jesus."

If I had time I could continue at length such quotations. Why did Mr. Smith bring Jefferson into this controversy anyway?

We are told that the Golden Rule "expresses enlightened self-interest." Can Mr. Smith give us a rule that will furnish better protection for the rights of others? A certain amount of interest in self is commendable. In the Golden Rule, and all other New Testament teachings, self-interest comes second to the interests of others. Jesus said:

> "Whosoever will be chief among you, let him be your servant; even as the Son of Man came not to be ministered unto, but to minister, and to give his life a ransom for many." (Mt. 20:28.)

Paul, in harmony with his Master's teaching, said:

> "Let no man seek his own, but every man another's wealth." (1 Cor. 10:24.)

Can Mr. Smith see any unwholesome self-interest in this teaching?

The charge that the Bible teaches the subjection of women comes with poor grace from Mr. Smith, after his having argued that women are in-ferior in intelligence. A sufficient answer is to remind him that it is in the countries where the Christian religion is accepted that woman occupies the highest position. Compare woman's position in the United States with her position in Japan. In the East Indies it was for a long time the custom to burn the widow alive on the funeral pyre of her dead husband. What stopped this custom? The introduction of Christian civilization by Great Britain. Before the Bible was introduced to the American Indians, their women were made to do all the hard work, and then occupy the coldest place in the wigwam.

The Bible lifts woman to her rightful place by man's side—his co-partner and helpmate.

> "There is neither Jew nor Greek, there is neither bond nor free, there is neither male nor female; for we are all one in Christ Jesus." (Gal. 3:28.)

Is the charge that the Bible sanctions intolerance of opinion, true? Jesus forbids us to judge our fellow men. (Mt. 7:1.) Paul, in the fourteenth and fifteenth chapters of Romans, advocates the most liberal attitude toward those who differ from us in matters of opinion. I quote a few of his statements:

> "One believeth that he may eat all things; another eateth herbs. Let not him that eateth despise him that eateth not; and let not him which eateth not judge him that eateth; for God hath received him." (14:2,3.)

> "One man esteemeth one day above another; another esteemeth every day alike. Let every man be fully persuaded in his own mind." (14:5.)

> "Let us not therefore judge one another any more; but judge this rather, that no man put a stumbling block or an occasion to fall in his brother's way." (14:13.)

> "Let us therefore follow after the things which make for his neighbor, for his good to edification. For even Christ pleased not himself." (15:2,3.)

Now to the arguments on eugenics: It is charged that Christians try to save people who are physically weak. Thanks for the compliment. Christians do not feel at liberty to take a man's life just because he is not physically strong. Christianity is not a brute philosophy; it deals with intellect and spirit, as well as flesh. Christianity does not place man on the level of a beast, and judge his value on a purely physical basis.

We are not discussing the question of legal sterilization of the physically unfit. Why avoid the main issue? Mr. Smith argued, in his tract, that for "the best male in a community to be the father of its children" would be the finest thing for the human race. I charged that this is immoral, vulgar and brutish. He does not deny the charge.

I do not know that Christianity opposes birth control, under certain conditions. An unnatural, illegal, mechanical birth control is opposed. I am not contending for the co-habitation of mental and physical defectives.

In reality, the issue is: shall we accept the atheistic "survival of the fittest," and kill all the weak—or let them die, without attempting to save them? Or, shall we follow the humanitarian program of Christianity, in helping the helpless?

The doctrine of "the survival of the fittest" is simply the old Iron Rule: "Might makes right." If I am stronger than you, and can, therefore, crush you, it is right for me to do so. Mr. Smith says the only standard of morals atheists have is based on "happiness here and now." I again ask him if it would be wrong, according to atheism, for me to knock a man unconscious and rob him. Judged by the atheist standard, if it contributed to my happiness "here and now," it would be right.

You will remember that I asked my opponent to tell us why it would be wrong to kill him. He offered no reason. He cannot offer a consistent reason. I suppose it is up to me to defend his right to live. I'll tell you why it would be wrong to kill him; he has an immortal spirit, made in the image of God, and in spite of the fact that he has degraded and deformed the soul God gave him, it is still wrong to take his life. Let Mr. Smith offer a reason why it would be wrong! Listen to him carefully, and see if he attempts it.

Denying the Biblical standard of manhood as he does, my friend cannot prove that he is a man. He cannot prove that he is not a hog. In order to give him a chance to refute it, I charge that he is a hog! Now deny it and offer your evidence, Sir!

In practice, if not in theory, the atheist recognizes a difference between men and animals. When an animal kills another of his species we do not try him in our courts. Why not? If a man, in a car, ran over Mr. Smith and injured him, he would probably sue the driver. If a horse kicked him, would he sue the horse? Even an atheist has more sense than that! What, then, is the difference? According to the atheist's theory, there is no difference between a man and a horse.

In closing, I maintain that I have fully established my charge that atheism is brutal, savage and immoral; that it offers nothing constructive, but is devastating in its results. Let me repeat: What must a man believe to be an atheist? Nothing. What must one do to be an atheist? Nothing. What must one be to be an atheist? Nothing!

Unintelligent Evolution vs. God and the Bible

(Friday evening, Aug. 16, 1929)

Proposition:

"All Things Exist as the Result of Evolution, Directed by No Intelligence."

Affirmative: Charles Smith.

Negative: W. L. Oliphant.

Chairman—F. L. Paisley.

Smith's First Affirmative

(Duration 50 minutes) Mr. Chairman, Ladies and Gentlemen, Honored Opponent:

I wish my opponent were in the lead. Since he is not, I ask him to let us know as soon as he has taken the floor, whether or not he is a Fundamentalist—whether or not he believed this earth and all that is in it, all the planets and stars were made some six thousand years ago, or whether he, too, has a little of that modernism that twists "days" to mean "periods." I ask also, if he has any questions that I have not sufficiently replied to, that he restate them; because I have only one more speech.

I am to present to you the case for Evolution, which, if established, proves that the Bible is not true. But I shall show you by the Bible itself that you cannot accept that book as the inspired word of God.

HISTORY OF EVOLUTION

I have not the time to give you the history of Evolution. It is sufficient to say it is an old doctrine. The Greeks knew of it when the Jews were ignorant barbarians in Asia Minor. In 1859 Charles Darwin established the truth of evolution by his "Origin of Species."

GEOLOGY

The star witness among the sciences for evolution is geology. Nature's museum, the earth's surface, contains incontrovertible evidence of the truth of evolution. In the stratified rocks one finds the remains of animals and plants which lived in the period when these rocks were formed. In the lower layers, there are no fossil remains. In the successive higher layers appear, first, the remains of the lower forms of life —early shell fish, snails, and coral, then fish, and on, in graduation, up to and including primitive man. The close relation between the fossil remains of successive layers cannot be accounted for except by direct descent.

Will my opponent explain why the fossil remains are found in that order? I give you Dr. Gladman's explanation. He is a Fundamentalist; and if the the Rev. Oliphant has a better theory, let him give it to us.

> "When God made Adam and Eve and the animals," says Dr. Gladman, "He made many models before he got just what he wanted, and these rejected models or skeletons were found *lying* around Eden. When the flood came they were scattered all over the world and became mixed with the universal mud, which hardened into rock, with the bones enclosed."

Coal is the fossil remains of dense forests. Who denies it, when the impressions of leaves and ferns are plainly visible? Who believes that coal veins a mile underground have formed within six thousand years? A lump of coal contains enough factual dynamite to blow the Bible to pieces. Chalk beds, some a mile thick, are the skeletons of small forms of life laid down on the bottom of the sea at the yearly rate of the thickness of a sheet of tissue paper, or one inch in a thousand years.

The Mississippi River has a delta where the mud has settled hundreds of feet thick in places. A hundred centuries was required for the formation. The Mississippi River once emptied into the gulf where Cairo, Illinois, now stands.

Niagara Falls has worn away twenty miles of rock. At the measured rate of three feet a year, that action would require thirty thousand years, not six thousand, as given in the word of God.

The Grand Canyon, a mile deep, has been carved through solid rock. Ages were required. Geology alone establishes evolution.

EMBRYOLOGY—DEVELOPMENT BEFORE BIRTH

The second proof of evolution it "Development Before Birth." In the course of development in the body of the mother, the unborn child passes through the various stages through which its ancestors evolved. At one stage it has the gill slits of the fish; at another, a tail longer than its hind legs; and at six months a thick coat of hair covering its body. In succession, the human embryo has the two-chambered heart of the fish; the three- chambered heart of the reptile, and the four-chambered heart of the mammal, which includes man.

I quote from Encyclopedia Britannica. Under the heading of Evolution, we read:

> "The fact that a fowl or a man passes through a stage in which its organization is essentially like that of a fish is meaningless, save on the assumption that land vertebrates (animals with a backbone) evolved from fish-like aquatic (water) ancestors."

The unborn baby undergoes changes in form as revolutionary as those of the frog, which, through cell and tadpole, reclimbs its line of descent. I ask my opponent why he denies descent from tailed beings of millions of years ago, when all persons, including my opponent, had a tail when in the embryonic stage. Why do not the Fundamentalists organize an Anti-Embryology Society? They could secure followers, and could perhaps get a charter in Arkansas or Mississippi.

VESTIGIAL (USELESS) ORGANS

The third proof of Evolution is the existence of useless organs within the human body. There are more than one hundred organs used by lower animals that are useless in man; including the appendix, the tonsils, the muscles for moving the scalp and ears. Every one has these; and some of you can use them—can move your ears and your scalp.

Every normal man has on his breast useless nipples. I ask my opponent to explain their presence, if they are not the remains of that which was once useful.

Every farm boy has seen the unused small toes of the hog, just back and above its big used toes. They were once useful. Charles Darwin compared these useless organs to the "b" in doubt, which is silent, but reveals something of the word's past, which at one time was sounded; just as the toe on the back of the hog's foot was once used.

SIMILARITY OF STRUCTURE

The fourth proof of Evolution is "Similarity of Structure." I quote Charles Darwin:

> "How inexplicable is the similar pattern of the hand of man, the foot of a dog, the wing of a bat, the flipper of the seal, on the doctrine of independent acts of creation! How simply explained on the principle of natural selection of successive slight variations in the diverging descendants from a single progenitor."

You will find the same general structure in man and the lower animals, which is easily explained on the principle of Evolution.

GEOGRAPHICAL GROUPING

The fifth proof is "Geographical Grouping." The animals in a region have the same general character; but when a barrier of an ocean or a mountain is passed, new forms of life are found. This fact cannot be reconciled with Special Creation. It necessarily follows from evolution. Until recently, Australia had none of the higher animals. Why? Because one hundred million years, ago, when the kangaroo was the highest form of life, Australia became an island. If my opponent believes the story of the flood, I ask him whether the kangaroo swam across the ocean to get to the ark.

MAN-MADE SPECIES

The sixth proof of Evolution is "Man-made Species." Man has created new species. The Burbank potato, grapefruit, and spineless cactus have been developed by artificial selection. The same process has produced two hundred breeds of tame pigeons. Ladies, I appeal to you especially, with this obvious and undeniable proof of evolution: Cabbage, kale, kohlrabi, collards, cauliflower and brussel sprouts have evolved from a common stock. You know the difference in these vegetables. They have been developed by man. What man does on a small scale, within a narrow range of time, Nature does on a large scale during geological epochs. Man's action is planned; Nature's is blind.

GRADATION OF ORGANISMS

The seventh proof of Evolution is "Gradation of Organisms." The divisions, or classes, are artificial. Species fade into species. Varieties are the beginning of new species. There is no definite line between plants and animals. I quote Huxley:

> "Certain questionable forms of sea life belong to a sort of biological no-man's land."

Two kinds of animals live today, the echidna and the duckbill, which lay *eggs* and yet suckle their young. Flying fish can stay in the air for one hundred yards. These are transitional forms.

Each organ of the body has an interesting history. Our arms and legs have developed from the belly fins of the ancient fishes. The Eustachian tube, connected with the ear, is the remnant of the gill-slits of the fish. The wrists are modified ankles of the forelegs.

Snakes are lizards without legs. Birds are flying reptiles, their feathers being modified scales. I appeal to you farm boys: Ask your Sunday School teacher and your preacher to explain why hens' legs are still covered with scales. These scales came through the reptile from the fish.

The earliest bird, the Archeopteryx, of which a well preserved fossil has been found, had teeth in both jaws and a long tail like a lizard and a wing with toes at the end. The wing is an evolved front leg.

The whale once had four legs and walked on land. It is a mammal—not a fish.

The history of the horse has been traced from a small five-toed ancestor, about the size of a fox. He walks today on the nail of his big middle toe.

Certain snakes have traces in their body of feet. Are these inherited from the snake which deceived Eve in the Garden of Eden? If so, per-haps someday traces of vocal organs will be found in the snake; for, according to the Scriptures, that animal talked, as well as walked.

MAN'S APE ANCESTRY

Now I come to a rather delicate subject: "Man's Ancestry." We atheists hold with Charles Darwin that man descends from the monkey. I quote from Darwin's "The Descent of Man," chapter six, next to the last paragraph:

> "The simiadae (ape family) then branched off into two great stems, the New World and the Old World monkeys; and from the latter, at a remote period, Man, the wonder and glory of the universe, proceeded."

Timid scientists or modernist clergymen who say Darwin never taught that man descends from the monkey, either are ignorant or they lie. That does not apply to my opponent; because he will admit, I suppose, that Charles Darwin taught monkey descent for man. If I had the time I would quote at length from the leading scientists within the last fifty years statements to the effect that man has evolved from the monkey. We issue a special leaflet on the subject, entitled "The Ape Ancestry of Man."

I have time to quote only a few of the authorities.

Haeckel:

> "From the half apes or lemurs, a direct line leads, through the baboons, to the anthropoid apes, and through these on to man."

Sir Arthur Keith, who, as an authority, dwarfs Moses to nothing:

> "Was Darwin right when he said that man, under the action of biological forces, which can be observed and measured, has been raised from a place among the anthropoid apes to that which he now occupies? The answer is 'Yes'!" Presidential Address, 1927.

Encyclopedia Britannica, Vol. 30, *page* 143, "Anthropology," by G. Elliott Smith:

"Comparative pathology, as well as the conclusive tests of blood relationship, has definitely established the fact of man's close kinship with the anthropoid apes, and especially with the gorilla."

See also "Man, Evolution of," in the New Supplement. The Jewish-Christian Bible is not to be compared with the Encyclopedia Britannica. Look up what the Encyclopedia Britannica says on the "Bible" and "Genesis," as well as "Evolution," "Anthropology," and Biology."

Ferris of Yale University:

"It is pretty well agreed that the anthropoid apes and man come from a common ancestor, and he in turn from some primitive, broad-nosed ape."

Huxley:

"Whatever organ we take, the difference between man and the anthropoid apes is less than the corresponding difference between the latter and the lower apes."

The difference are in degree only. There are similar differences between human beings.

Lull of Yale University:

"The gorilla and the chimpanzee are our next of kin"

Whoever denies kinship with animals should visit the Hall of the Age of Man in the American Museum of Natural History in New York, where, with his own eyes, he may see, arranged in rising order, the physical proof of that kinship, which far outweighs the stale hearsay of the Bible.

Why this violent dislike of ape ancestry? To have a criminal as a father is embarrassing; but who bothers about the character of his fiftieth grandfather?

Man is not yet fully adjusted to walking on his hind-legs. The frequent breaking down of the arches, the numerous cases of hernia and the difficulty with which children learn to walk, show that the upright position is new to man. The in-turned toes and the grasping and climbing ability of babies indicate monkey kinship.

Harelips, cleft palates, and the tails in human beings are throwbacks to earlier ancestral types. Cases are recorded of women with several pairs of breasts, with the nipples arranged in two rows, as in many lower animals.

THE BLOOD TEST

The strongest proof of man's ape ancestry is the blood test. If the bloods of two animals of the same family, such as the dog and fox, are mixed, no injury follows; but if the blood of a dog is mixed with that of a rabbit, the two kinds of blood cells fight for life. Human blood poisons and decomposes the blood of the lower monkeys and other mammals, but flows peacefully with that of the higher monkeys, or apes. The blood of man and the ape have the same chemical reactions. In other words, the orang, the chimpanzee, and the gorilla are not only the same as we are in structure, but are our blood relatives. In order to put this matter to a test, I challenge my opponent to have injected into his veins the blood of one of the lower animals; and I will have the blood of an ape injected into my veins. He will not accept, for he knows that I would live to preach his funeral.

How many of you here believe that the Chinaman, the negro and white man are descended from two Jews of six thousand years ago? Such differences would require one hundred thousand years to develop. Every normal person looks more like an ape than the Russian greyhound looks like a poodle dog. If man is made in the image of God, so is the monkey. If you doubt it, take a trip to the zoo. Why don't the Fundamentalists close up zoos? It should be against the law in anti-evolution states to exhibit monkeys.

Darwin, closing words of "The Descent of Man":

> "Man still bears in his bodily frame the indelible stamp of his lowly origin."

In the beginning was matter, which begat the ameba, which begat the worm, which begat the fish, which begat the amphibian, which begat the reptile, which begat the lower mammal, which begat the lemur, which begat the monkey, which begat man, who imaged God. This is the genealogy of man.

NO MISSING LINKS

The gap between man and ape has been bridged by fossils, of which the following, in the order of their discovery, are the more important: Neanderthal Man, 1856; Java Man, or Pithecanthropus erectus, 1891; who was so near midway that scientists debated whether he was a man or an ape; the Heidleberg Man, 1907; the Piltdown Man, 1911; and the Taungs skull or Australopithecus Africanus, discovered some fifty feet underground in South Africa, in 1924. There are no missing links.

Consider for a moment the alternative to the ape anceestry of man offered by the Fundamentalists. I wish I had the exhibits with me that I sometimes use. In a number of debates I have had a chimpanzee on the platform. If you don't like the ape as your ancestor; then, according to the Bible, you are descended from mud. Of course, you ladies would not like that, so we will give you something different. According to God's Word, you are descended from the rib of a man.

NATURAL SELECTION

What is causing all this religious hullabaloo over evolution? Natural Selection, the Great Theory of Descent. It is a mechanical process. It has five factors, as follows:

1.	Variation. No two plants or animals are exactly alike.
2.	Overbreeding. More organisms are born than can survive. As Malthus pointed out, animals multiply 2, 4, 8, 16; the food supply increases 2, 4, 6, 8.
3.	Struggle for Existence. Obvious.
4.	Survival of the Fittest. In the struggle for food and place, the weaker are weeded out. Nature kills those unadapted to their environment; the adapted, or fittest, survive.

5. Inheritance of Favorable Variation. If individuals reach maturity because of a favorable variation, those of their offspring which most inherit that variation will live to continue the race. In time this process of natural selection produces such differences in structure and use that

the resulting forms must be regarded as new species, genera, and finally, higher groups.

Whatever causes variation, natural selection determines survival.

I don't have time to give you in detail the working of selection. You can learn how the giraffe came to get its long neck, and how the other animals acquired various organs.

CONSEQUENCES OF EVOLUTION

What are the consequences of evolution? In the first place: Evolution bankrupts the Bible. It discredits the Word of God. The Law Scheme and the Scheme of Redemption do not go together. If descended from apes, we don't need a Saviour.

The second consequence of Evolution is to banish God from the universe. Prior to Darwin the clergy denounced this theory as the godless Law Scheme. Evolution is atheism; it substitutes natural law for supernatural intelligence. I quote Gladstone, the great English statesman—or politician, whichever you want to call him:

> "Upon the grounds of what is termed 'evolution,' God is relieved from the labor of creation; in the name of unchangeable laws, he is discharged from governing the world."

I think if you are honest you will agree with Gladstone. If you accept evolution, you must give up the Bible and God. I might say, in passing, that most Catholics reject evolution. The Catholic Church is practically a Fundamentalist organization, although it has few heretics. The Catholic Church has gone on record as saying man has not evolved; but in some Catholic schools evolution is taught as applied to the lower animals, though that's as contrary to the story of creation in Genesis, as is the evolution of man.

DISCREDITS DESIGN ARGUMENT

The principal consequence of evolution is that it discredits the only plausible argument the clergy ever had for the existence of God. I refer to the famous design argument. The animals in the North have a thicker fur than those of the South. Is it not more reasonable to hold with the atheist and evolutionist that this difference in thickness of fur is the result of the difference in climate than to imagine, with the clergy, that a heavenly tailor regulates the wearing apparel of the various animals? The old woman who thanked God for making rivers to run by populous towns had a theological mind. The clergy might as well praise their deity for making the bed of the river to fit the river, or making their legs just long enough to each the ground. Of course, there is fitness in nature. The continued existence of the unfit is inconceivable. The unfit must perish.

The priest or preacher reads his own feelings into nature. A tape-worm inside a human body night as well glorify God because his surroundings are so pleasant. A priestly worm would thank God for making man.

Goethe ridiculed the design argument by praising God for foreordaining the cork tree to furnish toppers for wine bottles.

If you believe in design, please observe how well God designed the diphtheria germ for killing babies. They nearly always kill when not defeated by man, and it is only in recent years that man can handle the situation.

I appeal to my opponent to tell us whether or not Caesarian operations discredit the design argument. It seems to me that a designer who would make a woman so she could become with child and yet be unable to give birth to the child; so that a doctor must cut the woman open to take the child out, is a poor designer.

Most organs in the body are imperfect. If God is a beginner, and this is his first world, I hope He improves with His next. Who designed God?

DARWIN AN ATHEIST

Darwin, in a letter to Dr. Asa Gray, said:

> "I see a bird which I want for food, take my gun and kill it. I do this designedly. An innocent and good man stands under a tree and is killed by a flash of lightning. Do you believe (and I should really like to hear) that God designedly killed that man? Many or most persons believe this: I can't and don't. If you believe so, do you believe when a swallow snaps up a gnat that

God designed that particular swallow should snap up that particular gnat at that particular instant? I believe that the man and the gnat are in the same predicament. If the death of neither man nor gnat is designed, I see no reason to believe that their first birth of production should be necessarily designed."

That is sound atheism.

If the Rev. Oliphant should fall into the sea; I don't hope he will do anything like this—but if he should, and should discover a man-eating shark headed his way, would he thank God for giving that shark so large a mouth? He probably would, but I suspect that he would wait until he reached shore. You ask a savage, "What makes a watch go?" and he will say, "A Spirit." You ask the preacher what makes the world go and he says, "A Spirit."

The idea of design arose when man's ignorance of nature permitted no other explanation.

From Charles Darwin:

> "The old argument from design in Nature, as given by Paley, which formerly seemed to me so conclusive, fails, now that the law of natural selection has been discovered."

Charles Darwin was an atheist. He did not care for the term and did not use it. He preferred the term "agnostic"; but he said to the great German Atheist, Buchner:

> "I am with you in thought, but prefer the word agnostic to atheist."

The agnostic is an atheist. See the definition of "Atheism," in the Encyclopedia Britannica, or any unabridged dictionary. Darwin had no God; he was an atheist.

BIBLE EXAMINED

So much for Evolution. I shall now take up the Bible. When you begin to examine that Book with an open mind you run across some startling facts. If you investigate, you will find that the Bible is one of twenty-seven books for which divine origin is claimed. Christians deny the divinity of all books except their own. We deny only one more than they. I would like to tell you how the Bible originated, how in part it was copied from heathen myths; and how the church fathers decided how many books should go into the Bible. They voted on the matter. There were three Christian Bibles. The Catholic Bible has more books than the Protestant. You have sixty-six in the one you use, and the Catholics have seventy-two. The Greek Catholics have more than that.

Here is something that preachers don't tell you. Martin Luther, who began the Reformation, and is the founder of Protestantism, rejected six books in the Bible. He rejected Esther, Jonah, Hebrews, James, Jude, and Revelation.

I quote from Thomas Jefferson concerning the book of Revelation:

> "It is between fifty and sixty years since I read the Apocalypse (Revelation) and I then considered it merely the ravings of a maniac—what has no meaning admits of no explanation."

The first five books of the Bible were not written by Moses. Their language did not exist in his age, and they also record his death and burial. Will Rev. Oliphant explain how a man can write up his own funeral? A biography of George Washington, wherein Lincoln is named could not be written by George Washington; and, by such proof, it is shown that the so-called books of Moses were not written by that individual.

I have not time to tell about all the myths, such as the Tower of Babel and the Creation—and where they came from. The Jews got them from the Egyptians and Babylonians almost word for word. The Babylonian first man was named Adami. After the book of Genesis, you find no reference to Adam and Eve.

The Higher Critics have won. Their victory makes the Fall of Man a fiction and the Atonement an absurdity. The descendants of apes don't need a saviour.

CONTRADICTIONS

The Bible contains two thousand contradictions:

> "Thou shalt not steal." Ex. 20; 15,

"Ye shall spoil the Egyptians." Ex. 3:22.

You know what the word "spoil" means. They spoiled them—stole their property.

"The wicked prosper."

In another place that is denied.

Satan provokes David to number Israel. I Chron. 21:1; and in another place God moves him to number them. II Sam. 24:1. Both accounts cannot be true; unless God and Satan are the same person. Whichever is true, God punishes neither Satan or David, but slays seventy thousand Israelites for the crime of being counted. (II Sam. 24:17):

"Lo, I have sinned—but these sheep, what have they done?"

Here is another contradiction:

"There is no respect of persons with God." (Rom. 2:11.)

But in Deut. 14:21, God authorizes the selling of diseased meat to strangers. If you have a hog that dies of cholera you can sell its meat to the stranger within your gates. Is not that "respect of persons"?

DOCTORED PASSAGES

There are quite a number of doctored passages in the Bible. It begins with a forgery. "In the beginning God," should read, "In the beginning the *gods.*" In Hebrew it is "elohim," and those who have been through the primary grades know "im" is the plural ending in Hebrew. Cherubim is the plural of "cherub."

I could give you a number of mistranslated passages. Matt. 3:2 is translated by Protestants: "Repent ye, for the kingdom of heaven is at hand."

The Catholics render it:

"Do penance."

The controverted word occurs fifty times in the New Testament. Which is right? How are you going to know?

ABSURDITIES

I want to give you an absurdity taken from the Word of God. The sun obligingly backs ten degrees to guarantee a fig poultice for Hezekiah. (II Kings 20:7-11.)

In the Bible you will find that the "Sons of God" cohabit with the "Daughters of Men," producing giants. (Gen. 6:4.) Who believes it? Hillbillies and uneducated persons.

In the new Testament you find another absurdity. Mark 11:12-22, records that Jesus cursed a fig tree for not bearing figs when it was not the season for figs. What would you think of a man who, in the early Spring, came to your orchard and finding there a barren fruit tree, should beat it down and curse it because it had no fruit on it? That is what your God did. Let the Rev. Oliphant explain the passage.

There are quite a number of impossibilities in the Bible. The Jews in Palestine were divided into small tribes. There were not many people. Yet, according to the Bible (II Chron. 13:17), five hundred thousand men, to say nothing of the women and children, were killed in one day, on one side. You know that could not have happened. At the great battle of Gettysburg in the Civil War, the dead numbered five thousand. That the Jews lost five hundred thousand men in one battle is preposterous.

BIBLE SCIENCE

Now, for the science of the Bible. Heaven is a solid roof supporting reservoirs of water. (Gen. 1:8.) The earth has foundations (Ps. 104:5), pillars (I Sam. 2:8), and four corners (Rev. 7:1). The rainbow is given as a pledge that the world would not be drowned again (Gen. 9:13). If you know anything about the nature of a rainbow, you know that it is as old as rain and sunshine. The Bible writer was ignorant of the nature of the rainbow.

Joshua stopped the sun and moon. I quote from Martin Luther:

> "The fool (Copernicus) wishes to reverse the entire science of astronomy. But sacred Scripture tells us that Joshua commanded the sun to stand still, and not the earth."

FULFILLED PROPHECY

You hear much about fulfilled prophecy. Jesus predicted his return within the lifetime of some of His hearers. (Matt. 16:28.) He is nineteen hundred years late. I ask my opponent when he thinks Jesus will return. Most of the true prophecies were written after the event. The Bible ends with an unfulfilled prophecy.

There are two stories of the creation in Genesis. They contradict each other. In the first story, trees are created before man; in the second, after *man.* I could give you other discrepancies, but have not the time.

There are two flood stories. In one, the animals went into the ark by twos; and in the other, by sevens. I ask the Rev. Oliphant which is true. Maybe two and seven are the same; three and one are the same in the New Testament, and perhaps in the Old Testament two and seven are the same.

CHARACTER OF BIBLE GOD

In the remaining few minutes let us consider the character of the Bible God. As Fundamentalists, you do not believe in a God who works through evolution. He is an impossibility. A god who would operate through countless centuries to produce a world such as ours shows a lamentable lack of intelligence. But can we accept the God of the Bible? If you will turn to Ex. 12:29-30, you will find that Jehovah (the Bible God) assassinates at midnight the first born of every Egyptian family. In II Sam. 12 and 14, you read that He kills a baby to punish its father for murder. David kills Uriah and God punishes David by killing a baby.

I read from I Sam. 2:3, Jehovah speaking:

> "Now go and smite the Amalekites, and utterly destroy all that they have, and spare them not, but slay both man and woman, infant and suckling."

Why this cruelty? Because the Amalekites had wronged the Israelites four hundred years before. In the fifth chapter of Numbers you will find God authorizes trial by ordeal. When a man suspects his wife of being unfaithful to him, he shall take her before the priest, who will give her bitter water to drink and if her belly swells and her thigh rots;

she is guilty. That is the divine method of determining whether or not a woman is virtuous.

Oliphant's First Reply

Mr. Chairman, Mr. Smith, Ladies and Gentlemen:

I am really pleased with the way my opponent starts off on this proposition. This is the first time, in my opinion, that he has presented a series of arguments really worth considering. I shall show my appreciation by refuting his arguments, one by one.

I shall notice first a few things said by Mr. Smith in former speeches, which I have overlooked. I want to answer now, because this is the last speech to which he will have a reply.

SINS OF BIBLE CHARACTERS

Reference has been made to *sins* committed by Abraham, David, and other Bible characters. Instead of these things proving the Bible to be an uninspired book, they are points on my side of the question. Books of fiction do not attribute crimes to their heroes. Even historians "color" their narratives according to their likes or dislikes. An un-inspired historian does not tell the bad filings about his hero. A biography written by a friend of the subject tells the good things; one written by an enemy stresses the weak points.

It is said that Hannibal, the powerful Carthaginian general who lived about 200 B. C., lost an eye in one of his perilous campaigns. Later, two artists were engaged to paint his portrait. They were anxious to please the general, and thought to do so they should hide his physical defect. One of them painted him full-faced, but gave him two good eyes; the other produced a profile view, carefully selecting the side which had the good eye. Their intentions were kind, but the result was in both cases a deception.

How different are the pictures given in the Bible! God does not shield even "faithful Abraham." The biographies of the Bible are true; if men committed sins, their sins are recorded. The fact that a book tells the truth should not be used as an argument against it. The Bible nowhere condones sin; where wrong is found in a life, God condemns it, regardless of who is the guilty party.

HOPE AND LOVE, ABSTRACTIONS

Mr. Smith criticizes my reference to hope and love being accepted by faith. I understand that these are abstract principles; but they exist, nevertheless. Why cannot faith exist, on the same basis? I also showed that we accept historical characters by faith. I again ask my opponent if he accepts the facts of history? If so, he exercises faith.

SIN AND DISEASE

Mr. Smith quotes me as saying that God sends disease as a punishment for sin. He misquotes me. God did not send disease into the world. Disease is one of the results of violation of law. Fire is a blessing to man, but it can also cause suffering. Some medicines are beneficial, if taken in proper quantities, but will produce death if too much is taken.

The germ theory (with reference to certain diseases) is now generally accepted by the medical fraternity. However, it is only a theory. We cannot afford to disregard facts, simply because they seem to conflict with theories—however general may be the acceptance of the theories. Physicians tell us that while they do not now know of any beneficial service done by certain bacteria; still, they are not willing to affirm that these germs, however parasitical they appear to be, have no beneficial purpose.

INNOCENT SUFFERS FOR GUILTY

We may not be able to understand exactly why the innocent must sometimes suffer for the guilty. Nature is such an intricate, complicated affair—every part so closely interwoven with every other part; that when "one member suffers," others must also suffer. The bearing of one another's burden sometimes requires the suffering of the innocent; and what a world this would be if none were willing to bear the burdens of others!

The atonement embraces this principle. Jesus did not have his life taken from Him; He voluntarily laid down, in the interest of humanity. (See John 10:18). The majesty of Divine Law must be maintained; and, at the same time, man needs mercy. As the loving parent willingly suffers for his child; so, the Christ voluntarily gave his life for mankind.

EVIL SPIRITS

Mr. Smith has much to say about the existence of witches, evil spirits, etc. That there were in Bible times, such things as evil spirits, no Bible believer can deny. I am of the opinion that they still exist. The Old Testament condemns witches. Whether these characters actually had the power to communicate with departed spirits, I do not know. It is possible that they only claimed such power. In either case, such persons stood in open rebellion to the law of God; and were to be punished for this wrong.

Modern Spiritualists make the same claim that was made by "witches" of Old Testament times, if any of them are able to do the things they pretend to do, such phenomena cannot be accounted for except as the work of evil spirits. We are not now living under the law of Moses, which prescribed the death penalty for witchcraft. Christianity is in no way to blame for the fanatical witch-burners of the Dark Ages.

FUNDAMENTALIST OR MODERNIST?

Mr. Smith asks whether I am a Fundamentalist or a Modernist. I answer, I am neither; I am a Christian, only. I am not obligated to defend Fundamentalism, Modernism, or any other "ism." As a "Christian only," I am at liberty to accept truth and reject error, wherever they are found. If Mr. Smith means to ask whether I believe the Bible to be the inspired Word of God, I gladly answer, that I do.

He asks whether I believe the earth was created six thousand years ago. Where does the Bible say the earth is only six thousand years old? We are told that "in the beginning, God created the heavens and the earth." So far as I know, the Bible does not tell us just how long ago the "beginning" was. Scientists do not know the age of the earth; it is certain that they do not know that it was created before "the beginning!"

DR. GLADMAN AND NEGRO REVIVAL

Mr. Smith seems to find it easier to constantly refer to his atheist-made Dr. Gladman than to deal in sensible arguments. For the same reason, he prefers to argue against the silly practices of a negro sectarian revival, instead of considering the intelligent worship of God, according to the New Testament. This is just an evasion of the issue.

He asks me to restate my questions and arguments, to which he has not replied. I could not possibly do that in the time I have; there are too many of them. I must now deal with his arguments for evolution.

EMBRYOLOGY—DEVELOPMENT BEFORE BIRTH

The recapitulation theory (that the embryos of higher animals pass through the various steps of development from lower animals) is a deduction from the theory of evolution, rather than a proof of the theory. Adam Sedgwick, Professor of Zoology, Imperial College of Science and Technology, London, says that it is even less than a mere "deduction." Hear him:

> "Thus the explanation ordinarily given to the embryonic structures referred to is purely a deduction from the evolution theory. Indeed, it is less than this, for all that can be said is something of this kind; if the evolution theory is true, then it is conceivable that the reason why the embryo of a bird passes through a stage in which its pharnyx presents some resemblance to that of a fish is that a remote ancestor of the bird possessed a pharnyx with lateral apertures such as are at present found in fishes...' (Encyclopedia Britannica, 11th Ed.,

Vol.. 10, pg. 322.)

The argument runs in a circle. It can be accepted only on the basis that evolution is true. Recapitulation is used to prove evolution, and then evolution is used to prove recapitulation! It reminds me of a conversation I once heard. One man said: "It will not rain until the weather gets cooler." Another said: "The weather will not get cooler until it rains."

Suppose we assume the theory that man evolved from the ape, how are we to explain, the fact that the shape of the embryonic ape's skull is more like that of a man's skull, than is the skull of the grown ape? If this proves anything, it is not that man evolved from the ape, but the converse; that the ape descended from man. Why are there no teeth in the embryo of the bird, since it is supposed to have evolved from animals which had teeth? There is no reason for calling the pharyngeal arches in the human embryo gill arches; they never develop into gills, such as the fish has.

While there are points of similarity between the embryos of various animals, these embryos are clearly distinguishable from each other at any period in their development. Furthermore, the embryo of each species always produces "after its kind." However similar they may appear, the embryo of the monkey develops into a monkey; and the human embryo into the human species.

There are certain organs in embryos that are distinctively embryonic and could never have functioned in adult forms. Prof. T. H. Morgan *says:*

> "It was recognized that many embryonic stages could not possibly represent ancestral animals. A young fish with a huge yolk sac attached could scarcely ever have led a happy, free life as an adult individual." (Critique of the Theory of Evolution, pg. 16.)

The recapitulation theory is rapidly falling into disrepute among scientists. The writer just quoted (an eminent evolutionist) says the idea that the embryo climbs its ancestral tree "is in principle false." (Evolution and Adaptation, pg. 83.)

Dr. W. B. Scott, of Princeton, in his "Readings in Evolution," pg. 173, speaking of this so-called "fundamental biogenetic law," says:

> "Nowadays, that 'fundamental law' is very seriously questioned and by some high authorities is altogether denied."

No less an authority than Professor A. Weber, of the University of Geneva, speaks of the "almost unanimous abandonment" of the theory. (Scientific American Monthly, February, 1921.) Karl Vogt, Geneva atheist, says:

> "This law, which I long held as well founded, is absolutely and radically false. Attentive study of embryology shows us, in fact, that embryos have their own conditions suitable to themselves, and very different from those of adults." (Quoted by G. B. O'Toole, Ph. D., S. T. D., in "The Case Against Evolution," page 276.)

Haeckel was perhaps the strongest advocate of the recapitulation theory. I showed you last night how he used fraud in his effort to prove the theory. Du Bois-Reymond made this caustic comment:

> "Man's pedigree, as drawn up by Haeckel, is worth about as much as is that of Homer's heroes, for critical historians." (Revue Scientifique, vol. 1, pg. 1101.)

It is manifest that embryos of the different species are not the *same*. Granting that they have points of resemblance; does this prove that one animal evolved from another? Is it not more reasonable to account for these similarities by supposing the Creator's work to be harmonious?

USELESS ORGANS

Mr. Smith contends that there are useless organs in man's body, and that these organs are holdovers from his animal ancestry. Before this argument is of any value, he must prove two things: First, he must prove that some of the organs in man's body are useless; and, Second, that the existence of such organs cannot be explained on any other hypothesis. He makes no effort to prove either of these propositions.

This argument has no foundation except in man's ignorance. The fact that the use of an organ is not known does not prove that it is useless.

Sir Arthur Keith, one of England's foremost scientists, and an evolutionist, says that "our list of 'useless' structures decreases as our stock of knowledge increases." ("Nature." December 12, 1925.) Huxley said, regarding these supposedly vestigial organs:

> "A cautious reasoner will probably rather explain such cases deductively from the doctrine of evolution than endeavor to support the doctrine of evolution by them. For it is almost impossible to prove that any, structure, however rudimentary, if it is in the slightest degree useful, there is no reason why, on the hypothesis of direct creation, it should not have been created." (Encyclopedia Britannica.)

Pineal Gland

The pineal gland is a little organ located in the roof of the third ventricle of the brain. Evolutionists have contended that it is the rudiment of a third eye, such as is found in certain lizards. However, it is now known that this organ is not useless. Arthur Keith, in his address as president of the British Association for the Advancement of Science, said:

> "We have hitherto regarded the pineal gland, little bigger than a grain of wheat and buried deeply in the brain, as a mere useless vestige of a medium or parietal eye, derived from some distant human ancestor in whom that eye was functional, but on the clinical and experimental evidence now rapidly accumulating we must assign to it a place in the machinery which controls the growth of the body." (Smithsonian Report, 1919, pg. 448.)

Dr. Swale Vincent, professor of Physiology, University of London, in his book, "Internal Secretion of the Ductless Glands" (1922), shows that the pineal gland has a very important function. He says that it seems to control the inflow and outflow of the cerebrospinal fluid of the third ventricle. (pages 385-393.)

Pituitary Body

Of this so-called useless organ, Dr. Vincent says:

> "For a long time the pituitary body was looked upon as a 'vestigial relic' and of no importance in the animal economy."

The writer then shows that it was discovered in 1906, that "the organ is essential for life." If it does not properly function it may cause what is known as "giantism" or overgrowth, or it may cause "infantilism" or small and defective growth. (Internal Secretion and the Ductless Glands, pgs. 264, 265.)

Thyroid Glands

The thyroid glands, located on either side of the windpipe just below the larynx, have been presented by evolutionists, as vestigal organs.

Dr. G. H. Parker, Zoologist of Harvard, says:

> "These have often been passed over as unimportant functionless organs whose presence was to be explained as an inheritance from some remote ancestor. But such a conception is far from correct." (Biology and Social Problems, 1914, pg. 43.)

It is now known that they perform an essential work in the body. In the dog and cat, their complete removal causes death. Dr. C. W. Salesby shows that the thyroid "creates a unique substance, mostly consisting of iodine," and that "without it, none can live." Without enough of this substance in the blood of an expectant mother, her life is imperiled, and her baby cannot be born normal. Dr. Salesby contends that if we will restore the missing iodine to our food, so that the thyroids "can live and work for us as they should," we will thereby "save a vast amount of ugliness, idiocy, deaf mutism, and possibly, cancer." (Quoted by F. E. Allen, in "Evolution in the Balances," pgs. 82, 83.)

Dr. Vincent says:

> "Defective thyroid function in the mother is the essential factor in the production of cretinism." (Glands, pg. 284.)

Dr. O'Toole says that these glands generate a hormone known as "thyroxin," which regulates the body temperature, growth of the body, etc. He also says:

> "Without a sufficient supply of this hormone,, the normal exercise of mental powers in human beings is impossible." (Case Against Evolution, pg. 294.)

Why doesn't Mr. Smith have some evolutionist doctor remove his thyroids? Or, has he already had them removed?

Mr. Smith likes to quote Thomas Huxley. It would do him good to heed Huxley's advice:

> "The recent discovery of the important part played by the thyroid gland should be a warning to all peculators about useless organs." (Quoted by F. E. Allen, in "Evolution in the Balances," pg. 86.)

The Thymus

The thymus, which is located in front of the heart and behind the breastbone, in the region between the two lungs, is a transitory organ. It is well developed at birth, but degenerates with the growth of the body. This has been considered a useless organ, but is now understood to have an influence on the growth of the bones. Ernest H.

Starling, Professor of Physiology, University College, London, says:

> "In certain cases of arrested development or of general weakness in young people, the thymus has been found persistent." (Physiology, Third Edition, 1920, pg. 1245.)

Dr. Albert Mathews says:

> "That they have an important function in the young animal, can hardly be doubted." (Physiological Chemistry, 1916, pg. 675.)

Islands of Langerhands

Until a few years ago it was thought by some that a part of the tissue in the pancreas composed of little projections about the size of a pinhead, and known as the Islands of Langerhands, was useless tissue. It was argued that this was vestigial structure left over from the lower animals.

The work of Banting and MacLeod, of Toronto, proved that this tissue plays an important part in the regulation of sugar in the blood, and thus in the prevention of diabetes. This discovery has led to the preparation of an insulin from the pancreas of animals, which is used in the treatment of diabetes.

The conclusions of Banting and MacLeod were verified in 1925 by the investigations of Drs. E. C. Dodds, F. Dickens and Swale Vincent. They say:

> "The result of this investigation was to provide further evidence that, as MacLeod states, the source of insulin is, in fact, the islet tissue." (Chemical and Physiological Properties of the Internal Secretions, pg. 53.)

The Appendix

Mr. Smith says the appendix is a useless organ. However, he is not an authority on this question. We shall hear Howard A. Kelly, M. D., LL. D., John Hopkins University; than whom there is no greater authority on surgery in America today. Dr. Kelly shows that the appendix is a valuable organ; that its secretion helps to lubricate the intestines. He says:

> "It increases the extent of the intestinal mucuous surface for secretion and absorption." (Vermiform Appendix, pg. 78.)

The Coccyx

My opponent contends that the coccyx in man is a remnant of a tail, and is, therefore, evidence of man's development from tailed beings. W. W. Keen reasoned this way in his book, "I Believe in God and in Evolution." In this book, he printed a picture of a "Head Hunter" of the Philippines, with a tail. He later learned and stated that the picture was a fake, "the tail having been added to the original by a photographer, I suppose as a joke." (Science, April 2, 1926, pg. 360.) It is to the credit of Mr. Keen that he was honest enough to correct the mistake. However, this honesty cannot be credited to atheism; Mr. Keen believes in God.

The coccyx serves for the attachment of several small muscles, which could not possibly function without it. Even Darwin admitted this. He confesses that the four vertebrae of the coccyx "are furnished with some small muscles." (Descent of Man.)

Professor A. Wilford Hall offers this testimony:

"Now, as regards the 'little tail of man,' about which Prof. Haeckel and Mr. Darwin have so much to say, and which is regarded by all evolutionists as such a powerful proof of man's descent from tailed ancestors, I wish to remark that a more manifest and inexcusable misconception was never harbored by men." (The Problem of Human Life, pg. 134.)

This author then explains that the spine of all vertebrates develops first, and the end protrudes until the fleshy portion develops to cover it. This explains the fact that this so-called tail is manifest in the embryo, and gradually disappears as the flesh grows over it.

I ask Mr. Smith how he accounts for the fact that the fish, which is not supposed to have developed from a tailed ancestor, also has this embryonic tail.

Extra Mammary Glands

It is cited that there are known cases of women having extra mammary glands, similar to lower animals. Professor D. Carazzi, in his Address of Inauguration in the Chair of Zoology and Comparative Anatomy at the University of Padua, says that these "supernumerary mammary glands are not a reversion to type." He says they have been known to develop "upon the median line, upon the deltoid, and even upon the knee, regions far-distant from the 'milk-line'." (Quoted by G. B. O'Toole, "The Case Against Evolution," pgs. 304, 305.)

Some of the evolutionist's "vestigial organs" are simply abnormalities. I once knew a boy who had an extra finger on one hand. Of what organ of the beast is this a relic?

MAN RIGHT-HANDED

As far back as we know anything about man, the right hand has, in general, been used in preference to the left. G. Elliot Smith says:

"The superiority of one hand is as old as mankind." (Smithsonian Report, 1912, pg. 570.)

On his theory that organs deteriorate with disuse, until, in course of time, they become mere remnants; how does Mr. Smith explain the fact that man's arms are equally developed? Bones, muscles, nerves, ligaments, tendons, blood vessels, and all parts are of equal size in both arms and both hands. The fact is that excessive exercise of a certain part of the body may overdevelop it, but this is an acquired characteristic; and is never transmitted to the offspring. The strength of the blacksmith's arm is not passed on to his children.

SIMILARITY OF STRUCTURE

Mr. Smith's next argument for evolution is on the similarity of structure between certain animals and man. We freely admit that there are many points of resemblance; but we insist that there are more differences between any species of animal and man than there are similarities. Dr. O'Toole quotes from Ranke, a long list of outstanding differences between the body of an ape and the body of a man. ("Case Against Evolution," *pgs.* 271- 273.) What do these radical differences prove?

Does the similarity of structure between the *ape* and man prove that man developed from the ape? When Mr. Smith sees a Ford and a Cadillac, does he think one developed from the other? There *are* many points of resemblance.

Frequently I read a book which reminds me of other books I have read. Do I conclude that this book must have evolved from the others? No; I decide that perhaps they were written by the same author. When I see that men and animals are made on more or less the same plan, I am reminded that they were all created by the same God. Is it not reasonable to suppose that, knowing animals and man were to breathe the same air, eat largely the same food and live under pretty much the *same* environment, a wise Creator would have made them somewhat alike in physical structure?

DIFFERENCE IN MENTAL CAPACITY

Man's superiority over the animal is very marked when we consider the difference in their capacity for mental development. For this reason man has been able to "subdue" the animal kingdom, as God commanded (Gen. 1:28). Animals do not make progress; the monkey has lived the same "monkey life" since the beginning of his existence. Man dwells alone in the field of advancement.

Speaking of the difference in man's brain and that of an ape, Dr. O'Toole says:

> "In the ape the brain weighs only 100th part of the weight of its body, whereas in man the brain has a weight equivalent to the 37th part of the weight of the human body. The cranial capacity of the largest apes ranges from 500 to 600 c. cm., while the average cranial capacity in man is 1500 c. cm. Moreover, the human brain is far more extensively convoluted within the brain-case than that of an ape, so much so that the surface or cortical area of the human brain is four times as great as that of the ape's brain." (Case Against Evolution, pg. 274)

NO MAN-MADE SPECIES

Mr. Smith says: "Man has created new species," and then offers the Burbank potato, grapefruit, spineless cactus, cabbage, collards, two hundred breeds of pigeons, etc., as examples. These are not new species; the Burbank potato is still a potato, the spineless cactus is still a cactus and the two hundred breeds of pigeons are all pigeons. None of these things have evolved out of their original species. Furthermore, these developments within species have been accomplished by intelligence. Does he think the accomplishments of Mr. Burbank were without intelligence? Sir, you should remember that you are affirming that evolution, "directed by no intelligence," is the creator. If the intelligence of man is necessary for development of plants and animals, even within their species; why do you contend that man developed from the lowest form of life without the direction of mind? He says that man's action is planned; while nature's is blind. Is it not strange that Nature has been able to accomplish so much more with her blind action, than man with his intelligent planning? We are told that there is "fitness in nature." Can there be fitness without intelligence?

If Mr. Smith's so-called man-made species are left without the care of man they degenerate—revert to original type. By selective breeding the small pony may be developed into the large Percheron horse; but when man ceases to guide the development, he reverts back to the common stock. We see that even development within species must be directed by intelligence.

Man's effort to cross different species has not resulted in the formation of new species, capable of reproducing themselves, and developing into still other species. The mule stands squarely across the path of the evolutionist at this point. Anah, grandson of the Horite Seer, reported the finding of mules in the wilderness of Horeb before the time of Moses. Thus, we see that the mule is not something "new under the sun." Why has not the mule continued in the process of species development? When species are crossed by man's work the hybrid, such as the mule, which cannot reproduce himself, is the result.

GRADATION OF ORGANISMS

My opponent's assertion that certain animals of the present time are transitional forms—connecting links between species, has no foundation in fact. Leading evolutionists admit that they know of no transitional forms. Professor Lull, in speaking of the evolution of mammals, says:

> "The record of the actual transition is as yet unrevealed."

In speaking of the evolution of birds, the same author says:

> "There is again no fossil record of transitional forms." (Evolution of the Earth, pages 128, 129.)

Even Darwin admitted,

> "There are two or three millions of species on the earth.... but it must be said today that in spite of all the efforts of trained observers, not one change of one species into another is on record." (Life and letters, vol. 3, pg. 25.)

If Mr. Smith has discovered connecting links between species, he has accomplished a feat at which evolutionist scientists, from Darwin to the present time, have balked.

I answered most of Mr. Smith's assertions along this line while discussing so-called vestigial remains, man-made species, etc. His gradations are purely fanciful. Take one of the examples he gives—the horse. He tells us that the horse has been traced from a small five-toed animal about the size of a fox. Even if this be true, it cannot be shown that the small animal, from which our present type of horse developed, was not a horse. However, the "tracing" to which he refers has been done very largely in the field of man's imagination.

James D. Dana, renowned geologist, in naming some of the animals found in what he terms the Champlain geological period, says that "the modern species of the horse was among them." He refers to them as "horses of large size." (The Geological Story, *pgs.* 267, 269.) Why has not the horse developed any since that time? Where is the proof that the horse was ever anything but a horse?

APE ANCESTRY

Evolutionists are not at all agreed as to just what animal is man's nearest relative. Darwin assigned to man and the ape a common ancestor, "the early progenitor of the whole simian stock, including man." (Descent of Man, *pgs.* 239, 240.) He said we might *"imagine three lines of descent proceeding from a common stock."*

I could quote from a number of evolutionists who do not think the ape is man's ancestor, but do not consider it worthwhile. One line of animal ancestry is as acceptable as another; the first step in tracing any of them is to (with Darwin) "imagine." There is absolutely no reliable proof of a bestial ancestry for humanity.

Mr. Smith says that if we do not accept the ape as an ancestor, we are descended from mud. Well, it might be interesting for him to learn that science has discovered almost every element of man's body in the earth. Oxygen, hydrogen, magnesium, sodium, phosphorus, silicon, carbon, etc—elements of the "dust," are also parts of man's body. Is this not evidence of the fact that "the Lord God formed man of the dust of the ground?" (Gen. 2:7.) God said to man:

"Dust thou art, and unto dust shalt thou return." (Gen. 3:19.)

We constantly see this truth demonstrated. We know that the body, after death, "returns to the dust." Can Mr. Smith give us such clear proof of man's having come from the ape?

Man is more than a material body. While his body is made of the dust, and returns to the dust, his spirit (that which God "breathed into him") returns to "God who gave it." (Eccl. 12:7.)

SIMILARITY OF BLOOD

Mr. Smith says the strongest proof of man's ape ancestry is the blood test. Suppose we examine this "strongest proof." In the first place—as Dr. Arthur I. Brown, surgeon, shows in his book, "Evolution and the Blood-Precipitation Test"—the so-called "blood tests" are not really tests of blood. He says:

> "It is necessary constantly to remember that what scientists are using in their so-called blood tests is nothing but serum—a small part of blood. If the blood cells are taken out of the blood, we have withdrawn a most important group of chemicals, in the absence of which, we are not testing blood at all."

According to the reports of evolutionists, the qualitative tests and the quantitative tests do not agree.

The qualitative tests reported by Prof. Nuttall, Lecturer in Bacteriology and Preventive Medicine at Cambridge, showed no difference between the blood of the crab and the lemur. Are we to conclude that the lemur (related to the ape tribe) is a close relative of the crab?

The quantitative tests also showed some very peculiar results. For instance, if these tests show relationship; the otter, jackal, sheep, ox, etc., bear considerable relationship to man. The ox, sheep and baboon produced the same results; while the whalebone whale, one species of baboon, the tiger, the African antelope and man all showed the same relationship. Does not this reduce the whole theory to an absurdity? Even Prof. W. B. Scott admits:

> "It could hardly be maintained that an ostrich and a parrot are more nearly allied than a wolf and a hyena, and yet that would be the inference from the blood tests." (Theory of Evolution, page 79.)

Dr. Erich Wassman, an authority on the blood, tells us that the blood-relationship between man and chimpanzee cannot be proved by similarity of blood until it has been shown that similarity of blood depends solely upon direct blood-relation between two animals possessing this blood. He then adds,

"And no one can maintain this to have been established."

Dr. Wassman points to the fact that, according to Friedenthal's experiments, the blood of the common crab, or that of a lug-worm, did not destroy the red blood-corpuscles of a sea-mew or a rat. He then concludes:

> "But surely no one would infer that for this reason rats must be descended from lug-worms, or sea-mews from crabs." (Modern Biology, pg. 458.)

Dr. Brown says the serum of the horse can be used with safety on a human being, but that this does not prove relationship between the horse and man; nor on the other hand, would incompatibility disprove it. He shows that there are no two men whose blood is of the same chemical composition.

Prof. H. Newman, who testified in favor of evolution at the Scopes trial, gives considerable time to the blood similarity argument; but admits that "there is no exactness about this parallel."

Dr. Brown also calls attention to the fact that asses' milk is more like human milk than is that of any other mammal. What does Mr. Smith think this similarity proves?

The truth of the matter is, that similarity of blood (or milk) proves nothing for my friend's position. Dr. H. C. Morton, well says

> "Ultra-microscopical examination of human and all animal blood has revealed difference of structure in the red blood corpuscles. No doubt this matter will be pursued; and meantime all that these blood—reaction tests prove (if indeed they prove anything) is blood similarity: and similarity does not involve relationship. It amounts to just this: That the blood of certain Primates and other mammals, share certain chemico-physiological properties. But chemical resemblance and identity of origin are quite distinct." (The Bankruptcy of Evolution, pg. 191.)

GEOLOGY

We come now to Mr. Smith's "Star Witness." What has geology to say for evolution? Nothing. Prof. George McCready Price, in his textbook, "The New Geology," shows that the arrangements of different kinds of rocks by older geologists was purely artificial and arbitrary. Facts that have since been emphasized, completely overthrow these artificial arrangements.

Some of the supposedly oldest strata of rocks are sometimes found above some of the youngest strata. Dr. Price gives numbers of instances of this reverse order, both in Europe and America. This reversal of order is found over areas containing as much as 20,000 square miles of territory. One of these areas begins in New York State, and stretches up into Canada. From these facts, Dr. Price has formulated what he calls, "the great law of conformable stratigraphic sequence," which he says may be stated as follows:

> "Any kind of fossiliferous bed whatever, 'young' or `old' may be found occurring conformably on any other fossiliferous beds, 'older' or 'younger.' "

He then adds that, this:

> "Forever puts an end to all evolutionary speculations about the order in which the various plants and animals have developed. —This law alone is sufficient to relegate the whole theory of organic evolution to the lumber room of science, there to become the amusement of the future students of the history of cosmological speculations." (Page 638.)

Thus we see that geology cannot tell us anything about the age of the earth. It does indicate that at some time in the distant past this old earth passed through some terrible catastrophe, which wrought a great change in its formation and life.

In northern Siberia there have been found the bodies of elephants frozen in the ice, so well preserved that dogs and wolves eat their flesh. Some of them have undigested food in their stomachs, and even bits of tropical plants in their mouths. Certainly there must have been some great change in the earth. Elephants do not live in frozen regions. The geologist Dana says that "the encasing in ice of huge elephants, and the perfect preservation of the flesh, shows that the cold finally became *suddenly* extreme, as of a single winter's night, and knew no relenting afterwards." (Manual, pg. 1007.)

Dr. Price accepts the Genesis account of the Flood as an explanation of this great change in the climate, life and surface of the earth. It seems that a universal flood would also account for certain ocean deposits now found between mountain ranges. How can they be explained in any other way? Certainly not on the basis of a gradual, evolutionary development!

Thus geology adds its testimony of the flood to that of history. Almost every nation has a tradition concerning the flood.

Geology Proves Degeneration

Instead of geology being a witness of evolution, it witnesses to a degeneration. Dana tells us that elephants, bears, hyenas, lions, etc., of the Champlain period were much larger than the present species. He says "these modern kinds are dwarfs in comparison." He says, "the Irish deer, skeletons of which have been found in Irish bogs, had a height to the tip of the antlers of 10 to 11 feet, and the span of the antlers *was* sometimes 12 feet." He tells of elephants "a third taller than the largest of modern elephants," and of rhinoceros eleven and a half feet long. He sums the matter up by saying

> "Thus the brute races of the middle Quaternary period on all the continents greatly exceeded the modern races in magnitude." (Geological Story, pg. 270.)

Where is the evidence for evolution in Mr. Smith's "Star Witness?"

MISSING LINKS

Evolutionists teach there have been classified as different species, 600,000 invertebrates and 36,000 vertebrates. If this is true, there are 636,000 unbridged gaps between distinct species. None of these gaps have ever been bridged.

My opponent says "the gap between man and ape has been bridged by fossils." He offers first:

The Neanderthal Man

This is a creature constructed on the basis of a few bones discovered in 1856. It has incited from competent authorities, a dozen or more different opinions concerning itself. Some have said it was a "human idiot," some "an old celt," "an old Hollander," etc., etc. (Case against Evolution: pg. 324.) James Dana says the capacity of the Neanderthal skull was seventy-five cubic inches "which is greater than in some existing men" (Geological Story, pg. 273).

Sir Arthur Keitl says:

> "We were compelled to admit that men of the modern type had been in existence long before the Neanderthal type." (The Antiquity of Man.)

Huxley said:

> "In no case can the Neanderthal bones be regarded as the remains of a human being intermediate between men and apes." (Evidence of Man's place in Nature, pg. 253.)

Dr. Thomas D. Parkman, Professor of Anatomy at Harvard, said:

> "The Neanderthal Man is not a specimen of a race arrested in its upward climb, but rather of a race thrown down from a still higher position." (Quoted by Dr. J. R. Stratton, in "Fundamentalist-Modernist Debates," pg. 96.)

Pithecanthropus Erectus

This name has been given to the creature manufactured from a part of a skull, part of a femur bone and a tooth, supposed to have been found by Dr. Eugene Dubois.

They were found scattered far apart in a gravel pit, along a rushing stream. (Smithsonian Report, 1898, pg. 447.) The femur bone was found a year after the finding of the bit of skull. Virchow, Dana, Klaatch, and other scientists rejected these bones as evidence of a "missing link." In the 1922 Edition of Encyclopedia Britannica (vol. 30, pg. 146), you will find in one short paragraph, three different opinions by three famous men, concerning these bones.

In 1894, twenty-four scientists met at London and made a critical examination of this so-called "missing link." Ten said they were the bones of an ape; seven declared they were the bones of a nan; while the remaining seven thought they were A some intermediate creature. Mr. Smith is certainly correct when he says that "scientists debated whether he was a man or an ape." Why, I ask, does he try to make us believe that he was neither?

Dr. Cunningham, of Dublin, one of the world's greatest authorities on Comparative Anatomy, said the bones could not have belonged to the same individual.

Heidelberg Man

Of this man (?) only one piece of a jaw-bone was found. He is one-half of one percent genuine, and ninety-nine and one-half percent restoration. As Mr. Francis D. Nichol remarks:

> "Evolutionists make great sport of the Genesis story that tells how a woman was made of a rib; and now, behold, they turn about and construct a whole man out of a jawbone!" (The San Francisco Debates on Evolution, pg. 76.)

Dr. Lull, of Yale University, says of the Heidelberg specimen:

> "The teeth are regularly placed and the canines are not in any way beastial in their development, less so, indeed, than in some modern men." (Quoted.by J. F. Herget, in "Questions Evolution Does Not Answer," pg. 65.)

Piltdown Man

This is but another specimen of the extravagant guesses of evolutionists. Four fragments of a skull-bone, a nasal-bone, a tooth and a bit of a jaw-bone were discovered. It was immediately "reconstructed" into a man. This first reconstruction was by Drs. Dawson and Woodward. The gave him a skull capacity of 1070 c.c. Later, he was "re-reconstructed" by Prof. Keith, who declared that his brain capacity should be something like 1500 c. c. This would raise him above some modern men in brain capacity. No "missing link" here.

Of the last named of Mr. Smith's "missing links," a skull found in Africa, Dr. Smith-Woodward says:

> "The skull is in some features the most primitive one that has ever been found; at the same time it has many points of resemblance to (or even identity with) that of modern man." (Science, quoted in Case Against Evolution, pg. 341.)

MAN NOT EVOLVED

After considering the various fossil remains of man, Professor Hugues Obermaier, says:

> "With absolute certainty, we can only say that man of the Quatenary period differed in no essential respect from man of the present day." (The Oldest Remains of the Human Body.)

Dr. Austin H. Clark, of the Smithsonian Institution, United States Museum, Washington, D.C., says:

> "So we see that the fossil record, the actual history of animal life upon the earth, bears us out in the assumption that at its very first appearance, animal life in its broader features was in essentially the same form as that in which we now know it." (The Quarterly Review of Biology, Animal Evolution.)

In the beginning God made man in His image, says the Bible; science has discovered nothing to indicate that this is untrue.

NATURAL SELECTION

Darwin's theory of Natural Selection has been discounted by modern science. John Burroughs, great Naturalist, says:

> *"Darwin* has already been shorn of his selection doctrines as completely as Samson was shorn of his locks." (Atlantic Monthly, Aug., 1920, pg. 237.)

The factors of selection mentioned by Mr. Smith fail him. "The survival of the fittest" doctrine does not take into account mental power; nor, does it consider the work of self-sacrifice. The "fittest" sometimes fails to survive because of sacrifice in the interest of those less fit. The World War destroyed many of the "most fit" men of the world.

The famous giraffe illustration fails. If only the giraffes with the longest necks had survived, the females would have all died; the male's neck is several inches longer than the female's.

If the inheritance of favorable variation aids evolution, what about unfavorable variation? That unfavorable variations have been inherited is shown by the larger specimens found in earlier periods.

CONSEQUENCES OF EVOLUTION

We are not interested in the consequences of evolution. Mr. Smith must first prove that evolution is true. If not true, it can be of no consequence. However, evolution—if true—would not eliminate the need of a Creator. It cannot account for the beginning of life, and there are evidences everywhere of intelligent design.

Mr. Smith compares the savage's answer that "A Spirit" made the watch with my belief that "A Spirit" made the world. Correct. The spirit of man designs the watch; but there must be a higher Spirit to design a world.

THE BIBLE

An honest comparison of the other twenty-six books which claim inspiration, with the Bible will convince anyone that they do not have the same grounds for their claim. The charge that the books of the Bible were first selected by the vote of a Church Council, is false.

The Pentateuch

It is charged that Moses could not have written the first five books of the Bible, since men, could not write in Moses' age. This is false. In Egypt we find that as early as 1385 B. C., letter-writing was in common practice among government officials, and there is a presumption that it was practiced even earlier. The Tell-el Amarna Letters are the correspondence of Egyptian allies in various places in Syria, embodying reports on the conditions of the various dependencies in their several districts. These letters cover a period from about 1385 to 1365 B. C. So we see that the art of writing was known in Egypt at least a hundred and fifty years before the Israelites left there. ("The Exploration of Egypt," pgs. 233-245)

Beginning shortly after the time the first five books of the Bible were written, we have quotations from them made by other writers. For centuries they were quoted, and every author of which we know anything attributed them to Moses. We prove that Moses was the author of the Pentateuch, and that it was written at the time claimed, in the same way we prove authorship and date of any other book.

The account of Moses' death may have been added by Joshua, or some other inspired man; or it may be a prophecy.

Creation, Flood, etc.

It is granted that other nations than the Hebrews have traditions concerning many things in Genesis; but is it not reasonable to suppose that these traditions were handed down from a common parentage— Adam and Eve? How does Mr. Smith account for the records of the various nations being so similar?

The fact that the Babylonians' first man was "Adami" merely shows that they learned about him from the same source as the Hebrews.

So-called Contradictions

Exodus, 20:15 and 3:22 do not contradict. The Israelites did not steal the goods of the Egyptians. The American Standard Version translates Exodus 3:22: "Every woman shall *ask* of her neighbor," instead of *borrow,* as the King James version *gives* it. That this is a correct translation is indicated by the Lord's statement in the 21st verse:

> "I will give this people favor in the sight of the Egyptians: and it shall come to pass that, and when ye go, ye shall not go empty."

The Israelites had been working for the Egyptians for centuries, without pay. God told them to "ask" remuneration for this service, and He put it into the hearts of the Egyptians to "give" it. Romans 2:11 and Deut 14:21 are not contradictory. God prohibited His chosen people from eating such meat; others were not prohibited from eating it. Then, possibly these animals were to be used in sacrifice. Jehovah would not accept such sacrifices; the heathen could sacrifice animals which "died of themselves," without violation of conscience. Anyway, God does not become a respector of persons in permitting men to buy what they want, with a full knowledge of what they are buying.

There is no contradiction between the creation stories of Genesis 1 and Genesis 3. The second account does not pretend to give the order of creation, but is simply a rehearsal of the creation history, without regard to order of occurrence.

Mr. Smith's supposed contradiction in the flood narrative is born of his failure to distinguish between clean and unclean animals.

When my opponent gives the *passages* which say that the wicked prosper, and that they do not prosper, we shall reply to this supposed contradiction.

Mistranslation

Mr. Smith says, "In the beginning, God," should be translated, "In the beginning, the gods," because the plural, "Elohim" is used. In the early Hebrew there was no distinction between the plural and singular form of a word. The plural of "majesty" occurs more than two thousand times in the Old Testament. In many instances the connection shows that it refers to only one. In Exodus 4:4, God said to Moses, "Thou shalt be to him (Aaron) as God." Here the plural is used, but will my opponent contend that Moses was more than one person? We also have evidence of the use of the plural form for the singular in meaning in the Tell-el Armana Letters.

However, the plural form may have been used in Genesis 1 with reference to the Trinity—God, Christ and the Holy Spirit.

There is very little difference in the meanings of the words "repent" and "penance." I am not responsible for the fact that the Catholics, in order to justify, their practices, have "colored" some passages in their translation.

I should like to ask how much Mr. Smith knows about the Hebrew language. Is he qualified as a critic of its translation?

Absurdities

The matter of the shadow on the sun dial going back, is not absurd when God is admitted. The man who makes a watch has the power to stop or start it, at will.

The Bible does not say giants were produced by the co-habitation of sons of God and daughters of men. It merely says, "There were giants in those days." (Genesis 6:4.) Geological records indicate the existence of a race of large men in some period of the past. We occasionally see giants now.

Mark 11:12-22 does not say why Jesus cursed the fig tree. The reason was supplied by Mr. Smith. We reject him as an authority!

Mr. Smith thinks it impossible that the Jews could have lost five hundred thousand men in battle. He should inform himself on the history of the Jews. Volney says that the population of Judea in the time of Titus must have been about four millions. ("Travels," Ch. 32).

The comparison between the battles of Israel and our battle of Gettysburg, is foolish. It should be remembered that Israel was a nation of great antiquity, while the United States was at the time of the Civil War, comparatively speaking, but *an infant.*

Science of the Bible

The Bible was not written as a textbook on any of the physical sciences. It makes no effort to explain things in the terms of science. Its language is the language of the people to whom it was written. However, where matters of science are incidentally mentioned, the statements are true.

It is now understood by scholars that the Hebrew word from which we get "firmament" in Genesis 1:8, means "expanse." The passage does not indicate that the heavens are a solid roof.

Modern writers speak of the earth's "foundation," "pillars," etc., without being charged with ignorance of science. These are every-day expressions in the language of any people. The word from which we get "corners" in Revelation 7:1 is not so translated in any other instance. It was used with reference to the four general directions, and does not signify literal "corners."

Genesis 9:13 does not say God made the rainbow at the time of the flood, but that he "set" it as a reminder of his covenant with man.

It is urged that the sun's standing still at Joshua's command is unscientific. A literal rendition reads, "Sun, be silent (or inactive.)" However, the Bible writer expressed that which, from the standpoint of the people, occurred. Mr. Smith has no hesitancy in speaking in that manner. He would say, "I saw a beautiful sunrise (or sunset)" while in fact he saw no such thing. What he really saw was an "earth-roll." That such an incident as Joshua's long day really occurred in the history of the world is fully proven from sources other than the Bible.

I now give Mr. Smith a few citations concerning the science of the Bible. Genesis 1:3 says there was light before the creation of the sun. For a long time infidels scoffed at this. Now scientists know that the sun is not the only source of light.

The rotundity of the earth is a comparatively new doctrine with us. The Bible says:

"He set a circle upon the face of the deep." (Proverbs, 8:27.)

Isaiah speaks of God as one, "Who sitteth upon the *circle* of the earth" (Isaiah 40:22). Jesus did not discuss matters of science per se; He came to teach people of a higher realm. However, that he knew of the globular shape of the earth, is shown in Luke 17:34-36. He says that at the time of his second coming—which will be instantaneous, one person will be sleeping, another will be grinding at the mill, while another will be working in the field. In other words, at the moment of His coming it will be night upon one part of the earth, early morning on another, and broad daylight in a third section of the earth. This could not be true except on the basis that the earth is round, and that it revolves. Job knew that the earth is poised in space (Job 26:7). Job also refers to the "empty place" in the north (26:7). At a comparatively recent date the Washington Observatory discovered that this is literally true. I ask Mr. Smith: How did Job know these scientific truths centuries before they were discovered by men of science?

The author of the 65th Psalm knew that light is vocal (verse 8). How did he know it? Job refers to the "way in which light dwells" (38:19). This reference is scientifically accurate. Why did not the Bible writer speak of the "place" in which light dwells? Because light does not dwell in a fixed place, but is due to the vibration of waves in the ether; traveling at the rate of one hundred eighty-six thousand miles per second, it may be said to dwell in a "way."

I should like to hear Mr. Smith explain how these Bible writers knew of these scientific principles thousands of years before they were discovered by scientists. We cannot account for this "advance information," in any other way than that the writers were not speaking from their own knowledge, but were *giving* a revelation from God.

Fulfilled Prophecy

The Bible abounds in prophecies which have been fulfilled. I might cite those concerning the perpetuity of the Jews. God said they would never be destroyed. (See Lev. 26:44; Num. 23:9, Gen. 28:15; Jer. 30:11; 46:28.) In spite of the fact that the Jew has no nation which he can call his own; no *flag* he can point to as the flag of his people; still, there are more Jews in the world today than there were in Christ's time The infidels, Volney, Gibbon, and others, bear witness to the fulfillment of the prophecies concerning Babylon, Tyre, Gaza, Ashkelon, Ashdod, Ekron, Ninevah, and many other Old Testament cities. Jesus, during His life on the earth, fulfilled more than four hundred prophecies of the Old Testament.

Mr. Smith says Jesus prophesied His return during the life of some of the disciples. A comparison of Mt. 16:28 with Mk. 9:1 and Jno. 14:15:20 shows that Jesus referred to His return in the person and power of the Holy Spirit. This was fulfilled on Pentecost (Acts, 2). When Mr. Smith scoffed at the idea of Christ's return, he did not know that he—an atheist, was acting in fulfillment of Bible prophecy. Listen to this prophecy:

> "Knowing this first, that there shall come in the last days scoffers, walking after their own lusts, and saying: Where is the promise of his coming? For since the fathers fell asleep, all things continue as they were from the beginning of the creation." (1 Pet. 3:3,4.)

We can no more judge the righteousness of the acts of God than a three-year-old child can understand all the actions of his parents. I do not know why God sometimes destroys nations. Probably the destruction of the Amalekites was a good thing for the world; I must leave that matter to the judgment of God.

Before Mr. Smith can justly charge God with punishing David's baby for the sins of David, he must see the other side of death, and know whether death was punishment to the baby. We know that it was a punishment to David to lose the child; while, in view of the Bible's teaching about life after death, it was a blessing to the baby.

Mr. Smith does not know that there was no scientific principle involved in the trial prescribed in Numbers, 5. Scientists believe the "truth serum" may reveal the guilt or innocence of a person. However, in this Bible case, the power need not have been in the "bitter water." The Lord operated in this case; if He chose to reveal guilt or innocence in this manner, puny man has no reason to object.

There are no conflicts between true science and true religion. Conflicts are the result of science misunderstood, or religion misinterpreted. The Bible is true; it has stood the test of time. If I had a title to property, and this title had been repeatedly tested for more than 1900 years, I should think my title good. The Christian's title "to mansions in the sky" has been contested for all the centuries of the Christian age: still it stands!

Smith's Second Affirmative

Mr. Chairman, Ladies and Gentlemen:

The Rev. Oliphant has repeated the statement that we accept on faith historical persons and characters, such as Napoleon and other great men. We have evidence of a different character for the existence of those individuals than we have for that of Jesus. There are contemporary records of those great men, but you cannot find a single passage (that is not admitted to be a later forgery) in a historian of the time Jesus was here, containing a single reference to that man. The gospels were written long after the time of Jesus.

It has been repeated that disease is caused by sin. If that is the way God works, why does he not so arrange that only the guilty should suffer. The Rev. Oliphant has never answered the question, "Did God make disease germs?" I ask for a definite answer. Either God made them or they evolved. Which happened?

He says there is no law without a lawmaker. That may appear to you to be profound. Did you ever know a lawmaker who did not have a father? Who is the father of your lawmaker?

I am not at all surprised to find my opponent, in defending that old book of his, professes a belief in Spiritualism. I have not time to refute that. I can only describe spiritualism as one of the greatest frauds ever perpetrated upon unsuspecting humanity.

He asks me to state where it says in the Bible that the world was created six thousand years ago. If you have studied your book, you know that the genealogy of Joseph, called the genealogy of Jesus, tells how long each man lived before begetting the next in the genealogical line. If you add the years, you get 4004 years back to Adam, who was made on a certain day of a certain week. Adam was made approximately six thousand years ago, and there were only so many days before that. My opponent has become a scripture-twisting Modernist. He stretches *"days"* into "periods." He knows that the world and the stars have been here longer than six thousand years. We now see the light from stars hundreds of billions of miles away. Those stars may have gone out of existence. They must have existed long before the time of Adam, or we could not see them today. Their light would not have reached us.

My opponent seeks to give the impression that scientists have rejected evolution, that they don't believe in it any more. He misleads you. There is not a scientific association in the more enlightened countries whose members are not almost unanimous in accepting evolution. They disagree only as to details and methods. The American Association for the Advancement of Science came out squarely for evolution at its convention in 1922. It was meeting in Cambridge, Massachusetts, the home of the Harvard University. The association officially declared:

> "No scientific generalization is more strongly supported by thoroughly tested evidence than is that of organic evolution."

The scientists quoted by my opponent are either dead men or living nobodies. Who is Arthur Brown? And this man Price? What position do they hold? Why does he not show you some learned opponents of evolution? He picks out a man here and there and yonder of whom we have never heard.

He quotes Sir Arthur Keith. The quotation is correct; but did he tell you that Keith is one of the foremost advocates of the ape ancestry of man? He was President of the British Association for the

Advancement of Science. Almost the entire scientific world champions evolution. And what has my opponent to show? An individual here, and a professor there, and a man dead long ago—and not known well when alive.

I have not time to go into the controversy concerning Haeckel; but it is conceded that the scientists exonerated him. If you want to know the truth of the matter, read the pamphlet by Haeckel —his answer to the Jesuits.

Evolution is the universal question—answered. Why can some persons wiggle their ears? Why do we have buttons on our coats? Why does every person have hair on his body? Why are there silent letters in the English language? Only evolution answers. Why do the Jews refuse to eat pork? Because at one time they worshipped the wild boar. Why do Christians shut their eyes while praying? Because their religion has evolved from sun worship, and they naturally closed their eyes while facing the sun.

The Rev. Oliphant tells you Evolution left to itself proceeds by degeneration. I want to ask him whether, in his opinion, any species have disappeared. If his theory be true, there were more species at the beginning than there are today. I wonder if he believes that.

The Rev. Oliphant asks if you can have fitness without intelligence. In the nature of the case, unfitness cannot continue to exist. I tear here a piece of paper. (Here the speaker picked up a piece of paper, tore it in two, and then put the pieces together.) I put it back. Does it not fit? Of course. Was there any intelligence in the tearing of the paper? Certainly not. The clergy might as well say that intelligence made my legs just long enough to reach the floor.

My opponent does not believe the books of the Bible were accepted by vote. Will he tell us how they were accepted? When the church councils were held, maybe the meetings were Bolsheviki. No, they accepted them by vote. He says the spoiling of the Egyptians was not stealing. It was getting money under false pretenses. What is the difference? He asks for the citation about the wicked prospering. See Job 21:37. Eccl. 8:13 teaches the contrary. He asked for other passages. I cannot give them now, for lack of time.

It is denied that there is a contradiction in the flood story. If you will look that up you will find that according to the so-called Word of God, the animals went into the ark by twos and sevens —both the clean and the unclean; and it is not true as he explained. There is no argument. Look it up. Gen. 7:2 and 7:8-9.

Certain passages have been quoted from Job trying to show that the Jews knew that the world was round. The author of Job may have so known; but I doubt it. Job is not a Jewish book, and is so recognized by the scholars in the seminaries.

I ask those of you who believe that the book of Job is inspired, to read the 7th chapter, 9th verse:

> "As the cloud is consumed and vanisheth away; so he that goeth down to the grave shall come up no more."

The doctrine of immortality was unknown to the Jews until the time of the New Testament. It is not in the Old Testament. Why was it Job did not know he would live after he died? Hear the wise man, Eccl. 9:5:

> "The dead know not anything, neither have they any more a reward."

Let's hear Ecclesiastes again, the inspired word of God:

> "There is no knowledge or wisdom in the grave, where man goeth."

My friend has referred a number of times to Professor Millikan, and other scientists, as holding that there is no conflict between science and religion. Does he mean the Christian religion? Does he seek to give you the impression that such men as Millikan and other scientists whom he named, believe such tales as the virgin birth, the resurrection, the story of Adam and Eve, the Flood, and all those fables in the Old Testament? They do not, and he should have told you.

I have only a moment or so in which to conclude. My opponent has admitted he cannot comprehend God nor explain him; that he does not know where Heaven is; how far it is, or in what direction it lies. He is selling you a gold brick. What did this God of his do? How does he help you? Where did he ever do anything?

The action of God in this world is very much like that of the stone with which you can make white stone soup. Here is the recipe for making this delicious dish: To the white stone, add some meat and some vegetables, together with the right seasoning. Cook properly and you have a wonderful soup.

Do everything needed to be done, and then credit God with the results —that's religion!

Oliphant's Second Reply

Brother Chairman, Ladies and Gentlemen, Mr. Smith:

This is the last speech in this discussion. I cannot, of course, introduce any new arguments. Although we have no rules governing this debate, I shall not be unfair to my opponent. I wish that we had more time; there are so many more arguments I should like to have made. In the few minutes at my command I can do no more than give you a brief reiteration of the things to which you have already listened.

In our first proposition, I showed that we cannot explain the origin of life, the origin of consciousness, or the beginning of man's moral nature, without God. In fact, atheism does not account for the beginning of anything. My friend has offered tonight the only alternative to my contention that God is creator. What is this alternative? It is chance—evolution "directed by no intelligence." His substitute fails; first, because he has not proved that it is true; and second, because—if true—it does not account for things as they are. How can any intelligent person believe that the orderly universe which man beholds, is the result of the working of blind chance—a mere "fortuitous concourse of atoms?"

Referring to his paper-tearing illustration, Mr. Smith says this is an example of "fitness without intelligence." He declares there was no intelligence back of the tearing of the paper. Perhaps not, since he did the tearing; if you had done it, there would have been intelligence used. However, Mr. Smith also used intelligence. He tore the paper according to design previously fixed in his mind. It had to be fitted back together according to plan; otherwise it would not fit. This would be all the more evident had the paper been torn several times; the various pieces, in order to fit, must be put together intelligently. Can we believe that such a harmonious fitting together of all the "pieces" of the universe is without the work of mind?

I quoted a number of imminent scientists who say that science cannot account for the beginning of life. We are unable to imitate the original life-producing process. If it could be shown that evolution explains the intricate forms of life we now have, it would still be at a loss to show how the original germ of life came to exist.

It is true that I cannot comprehend God; nor can I comprehend the principle of life. The most ignorant man can plant a seed in the earth, and watch it grow into a plant; while the wisest man in the world cannot explain the life-germ in the tiny seed.

It is charged that I have not introduced any real scientists who do not believe in evolution. To say one believes in evolution does not necessarily mean that he believes what Mr. Smith is advocating. We all believe in evolution, in one sense of the word. We know that there is development within species. What we are denying is that one kind of life develops into a distinctly different kind.

It is true that the American Association for the Advancement of Science passed resolutions in favor of the evolution hypothesis. These men also engaged in some very unscientific, and undignified language concerning W. J. Bryan, and his "Round Head" adherents. Dr. O'Toole says the meeting at which these resolutions were passed "was but sparsely attended, and packed, for the most part, with the ultra-partisans of transformism." (Case against Evolution, pg. 343.) Even this "ultra-partisan" group did not claim that evolution is more than a theory.

Honest scientists are often wrong. The theories of science are constantly changing. Dr. Frank Allen, head of the Department of

Physics, University of Manitoba, recently said:

> "There is scarcely a theory of science which is generally accepted today, of which I would be ready to affirm that it may not be abandoned within a few years. Nearly all of the theories which were regarded as satisfactory a few years ago, are now either modified or discarded by scientists." (Evolution in the Balances, pg. 182.)

It is not true that all scientists accept the theory of evolution. I mention Dr. Clark Wissler, Curator-in-Chief of the Anthropological section of the American Museum, New York City; Prof. W. Brance, Director of the Institute of Geology and Palaentology, University of Berlin; Sir Wm. Dawson, President, McGill University; Dr. Howard A. Kelly, John Hopkins University; Prof. L. S. Beale, King's College, London; Dr. Etheridge, Curator of the Natural History Museum; Dr. Austin H. Clark, Smithsonian Institution, United States Museum. These eminent scientists, and many others that could be named, reject the theory of evolution. The last named, Dr. Clark, who is probably second to no other scientist in ability, says:

> "Thus so far as it concerns the major groups of animals, the creationists seem to have the better of the argument. There is not the slightest evidence that any one of the major groups arose from any other." (Quarterly Review of Biology.)

Many of those who accept evolution regard it as no more than a theory, which can be accepted only by faith. Dr. L. T. Moore, of the University of Cincinnati, says:

> "The more one studies paleontology, the more certain one becomes that evolution is based on faith alone; exactly the same sort of faith which it is necessary to have when one encounters the great mysteries of religion." (Princeton Lectures, pg. 160.)

Mr. Smith charges that Dr. Price is a "nobody," and that no scholars agree with his geological theories. Mr. Price is a member of the American Society for the Advancement of Science. His theory of geology was introduced in his book, "Illogical Geology." I know of the following scholars who endorsed the book:

- Prof. William C. Wilkinson, University of Chicago: C. W. Hall, Professor of Geology and Mineralogy, University of Minnesota;
- Wm. G. Moorehead, President, Xenia Theological Seminary;
- Prof. Luther T. Townsend, Boston University;
- Prof. James Orr, United Free Church College, Scotland;
- Prof. George H. Parker, Department of Zoology, Harvard University;
- Prof. A. H. Sayce, Oxford University, England; and
- Prof. Franklin Johnson, University of Chicago.

I am sure many more endorsed it. Even Dr. David Starr Jordan, President, Leland Stanford University, said: "It is a very clever book." Those who do not accept Mr. Price's position find it easier to laugh at his arguments than to answer them. Scientists do not agree in their conjectures about the age of the earth. It has been estimated all the way from six or seven thousand years, up to 10,000 million years. If you ask: Does the Bible agree with science as to the age of the earth? I ask: What science? It is evident that the Bible could not agree with all these estimates.

However, the Bible does not tell us the earth's age. I do not know whether the six days of Genesis were six literal days, or six long periods of time. The term "day" is frequently used to designate an indefinite period. This may have been the sense in which it was used in Genesis. I do not think it does the Bible record any injury to think they were long periods of time. I do not know that the six days of Genesis even relate to the original creation. It may be that all we know of the creation is that which we are told in the first verse of the Bible. The work of the six days may have been done long after the creation. There is no need to argue these questions. Opponents of the Bible have nothing to offer but a guess. No scientist will contend that he *knows* anything about the age of the earth. I believe the Bible account, regardless of what period of time is meant by "day." Nothing has been offered to shake our faith in the Bible record.

Mr. Smith repeats the charge that we do not know what books the Bible should contain, except by the vote of a church conference. The earliest church assembly to catalogue the books of the New Testament was the Council of Carthage, which met in A. D. 397. Catalogues of the New Testament had been made by numbers of individuals before this date. Athanasius, who was Bishop of Alexandria from 326 to 373 A. D., lists all the books of the New Testament as we have them today. Cyril, who was Bishop of Jerusalem, catalogued the books of the New Testament. He lived from 315 to 386 A. D. Several other men who lived before any church council passed on the genuineness of Bible books, prepared lists of the books of our New Testament.

Christians of the first four centuries quoted from the books of the New Testament. These quotations were so many and so copious that if the New Testament were lost, it could be reproduced from these writings. Some of these early writers were: Eusebius (207-340 A. D.), Origen (185 to 254), Clement of Alexandria (165 to 230), Irenaeus (135 to 200), Polycarp (disciple of the Apostle John). All these, and many others, quoted from the books of the New Testament, and attributed them to the authors whose names they now bear. When the church councils, later, made catalogues, they were governed by the acceptance and use of the books from the time of the apostles.

Mr. Smith seems to insinuate that Jesus is not a historical character. Not even an infidel of any standing has ever questioned the facts that Jesus lived at the time the gospel writers say He did, and that He did many of the things ascribed to Him in the gospels. Tacitus, a reputable Roman historian, who was born about 58 A. D. tells us that Christians "derived their name and origin from Christ, who, in the reign of Tiberius, had suffered death by the sentence of the procurator Pontius Pilate." (Annals, XV, 44).

Pliny, who was born about 62 A. D., tells of the punishment of Christians, and indicates that he understood Christianity to have originated with Christ. (Letter to the Emporer Trajan, Quoted by Gibbon, Vol. 2, *Pgs*. 26, 27).

Suetonius, Secretary under the Emperor Adrian, was born about 68 A. D. This writer says that Christians were punished, and that Chrestus (Christ) was their leader. (Lives of the Twelve Caesars).

Celsus was an early opponent of Christianity. He wrote a book, "The True Word," in which he not only admits that Jesus lived, but that He performed miracles.

We might also refer to the celebrated passage from Josephus:

"Now there was about this time Jesus, a wise man, if it be lawful to call him a man, for he was a doer of wonderful works —He was (the) Christ; and when Pilate, at the suggestion of the principal men amongst us, had condemned him to the cross, those that loved him at the first did not forsake him, for he appeared to them alive again the third day, as the divine prophets had foretold these and ten thousand other wonderful things concerning him: and the tribe of Christians, so named from him, are not extinct at this day." (Antiquities, Bk. 18, chap. 3).

I am aware that the genuineness of this passage has been questioned, However, there have been infidels in all ages who have accepted it. Ernest Renan said: "I think the passage on Jesus authentic" (Life of Jesus, pg. 13). Even the atheist, Joseph McCabe, thinks Josephus mentioned Christ, but that the passage was altered by some Christian hand at a later date. Mr. McCabe, though a radical atheist, accepts the historicity of Jesus. (See his book, "Did Jesus Ever Live?"). If we grant that this passage is spurious, we still have a reference to Jesus by Josephus. In his Antiquities, book 20, chapter 9, while discussing the death of James, Josephus refers to "Jesus, who was called the Christ."

If it were conceded that Jesus did not live, we would have to attribute Divinity to the gospel writers. Men who could imagine such a character must have been more than mere men. He who denies the life of Jesus as given by the Evangelists has more to account for than we, who accept their accounts. It would take a "Christ" to imagine the Christ of the gospels.

All the evidence I have offered is from men who were not favorable to Jesus. The testimonies of many Christian historians could be offered.

Mr. Smith says Job may have known the scientific truths which he stated. I again ask, how could Job have known these things, without inspiration?

The passage my opponent quoted from Job in regard to the resurrection is a part of Job's complaint, which runs throughout the first part of the book. After the Lord "answered Job out of the whirlwind," his attitude was completely changed. Hear his confession:

"Then Job answered the Lord, and said, I know that thou canst do everything (even to raising the dead—Oliphant) and that no thought can be withholden from thee..... I uttered that I understood not; things too wonderful for me, which I knew not.... where- fore I abhor myself, and repent in dust and ashes." (Job, 42:1-6).

The Bible is an inspired book; its record of facts is correct. There are quotations in the Bible, which do not state the truth. The fact that the statements were made, is recorded by Inspiration. For instance, the words of Satan are sometimes quoted. The Holy Spirit does not vouch for the truthfulness of the statements; but the writer was inspired in his telling of Satan's *having made them.* So, we have in the book of Job, some statements made by Job, Eliphaz, Bildad and Zophar, which may not be true. Job realized that he had made some false statements; hence, made the confession I quoted from him. The charge that Job did not know of the resurrection is false. Read the nineteenth chapter, verse twenty-six:

"Though after my skin worms destroy this body, yet in my flesh shall I see God."

Mr. Smith quotes Solomon's statement that there is no knowledge in the grave. Certainly, there is not. Who has ever contended that there is knowledge in the grave. Only the body of man goes to the grave. The same writer says, "the spirit shall return unto God." (Eccl. 12:7) The part of man that "knows" is never in the grave. My friend quotes a part of Eccl. 9:5 "The dead know not anything, neither have they any more a reward." Why did he not quote the rest of the passage? The sixth verse closes with a qualifying clause: "in anything that is done *under the sun."* In other words, the dead know nothing, have no reward, etc., "under the sun" (upon the earth). You can take any book, and make it teach *anything;* provided you cut its sentences up in such manner. Infidels do not deal honestly with the Bible.

God did not introduce slavery (Ex. 21), as my opponent has charged; on the contrary, God here limits slavery, and provides a way for a slave to become a free-man. All nations of that ancient time practiced slavery. God showed His displeasure at the practice, by gradually leading His people out of it. It would have been unwise to have attempted to suddenly abolish such a universal custom. God reveals Himself and His laws to man as rapidly as man is capable of receiving them. Man's receptive capacity limits God's revelation. When Stanley was in the jungle of Africa, the pigmies asked him where he came from and how he got there. Having never seen a ship or an ocean, their vocabulary contained no words for ships or oceans. Hence Stanley was unable to answer their question. His inability was not due to his lack of knowledge, but to, the natives' lack of understanding. So, if our revelation of God is not clear, it is because of our lack of receptive capacity.

Job, 21 and Eccl. 8 do not contradict. Job does not teach that the wicked prosper, in the long run. Verse 30 *says* that the wicked are "reserved to the day of destruction." The passage teaches that, though the wicked may seem to prosper, temporarily; they must eventually reap what they sow. Ecclesiastes teaches the same truth. I am re minded of this story: An infidel wrote an article for a country newspaper, in which he said: "Your God does not punish men for wrong. I plowed my land on Sunday, planted my corn on Sunday and harvested it on Sunday. This October, I have as much corn as any of my neighbors, who went to church on Sunday." The editor printed the article, and followed it with this brief reply: "God does not settle all His accounts in October."

There is no contradiction in the Genesis account of the flood. In Gen. 7:2, God is telling Noah how many clean and unclean animals to take into the ark. The eighth and ninth verses tell how they went in, "by twos and twos"—not how *many* went in.

Throughout the debate yesterday afternoon, I challenged my opponent to give us the atheist's standard of morality. I charged that, according to the only rule he offered, it would not be wrong to rob or kill. He never denied my charge. I asked him to offer any reason why it would be wrong for me to take his life; he offered none. Why? Because, according to atheism, it is no more wrong to kill a man than it is to kill a beast. I charged that atheism is brutal, savage and immoral; he did not so much as deny the charge. It, therefore, stands, as I made it.

I charged that atheists have never built a school or a hospital. He denied the charge. I asked him to name such an institution, which was built by atheists. The debate now closes without his having named a single one. He could not do so, for the simple reason that, there is no such institution. I showed that even the school Mr. Smith attended was built by religion. Sir, you are biting the hand that feeds you!

I wish it to be remembered that Mr. Smith does not deny that his position means the killing of persons who are physically weak. Such is the brutal theory he wants to establish in the place of God and His word. So long as there are intelligent men and women in the world, he cannot succeed.

There are no contradictions in the Bible. I think I have shown that none of his supposed conflicts are real; but suppose I cannot prove that there are no contradictions in God's word: what does that indicate? Merely that I do not understand all about Infinite things. God has nowhere said that, from man's viewpoint, there are no contradictions in His word. Nature is made up of opposites and contraries. We have opposite sexes; opposite forces (centripetal and centrifugal), constantly pulling against each other; cold and heat; darkness and light; etc. If I fail to harmonize all the statements of the Bible, it still looks much like God's other Book—Nature.

Music is made up of notes; but if these notes are jumbled and mixed, without design, hideous and contradictory sounds are produced. So, the Bible sings a beautiful song of eternal life to the man who conscientiously studies it; to the disbeliever who distorts its notes, it presents a discord. It is not the Bible scholar who finds contradictions in the Bible.

The Bible has builded itself into the very warp and woof of our being. Its influence on our literature is remarkable. Take Shakespeare: I found 138 references to Bible characters, and 53 references to Bible incidents, facts, places, etc., in his works. He also has about 190 passages which are parallel with Bible statements. If the Bible were destroyed, it could probably be reproduced from the literature of our day.

A ten-year-old book on science is hard to find; books of fiction are out-of-date in a few years; but the Bible is still the "best seller." During 1927, the American Bible Society distributed 10,034,797 copies of the Bible. This society is 112 years old. Since the date of its organization it has averaged three volumes a minute, night and day—making a total of 194,063,757 volumes distributed since its work began. This is an average of 197 copies an hour for 112 years. Its average production now is 27,492 copies a day, 1,145 an hour, or 19 a minute. This society has circulated the Scriptures in 250 languages and dialects. It has been estimated that if all the persons who have received copies of the Scripture from this one agency were to stand in line, the line would reach four times around the world. Does this look like the Bible is losing its popularity.

The Bible has been bitterly fought in every century of its life; still it lives. It is adapted to the needs of humanity; it furnishes guidance, hope and cheer to, an otherwise, cheerless world. All the hope the infidel has in life comes, indirectly, from its pages. Col. Ingersoll, at his brother's grave, said:

> "Life is a narrow vale between the cold and barren peaks of two eternities. We, strive in vain to look beyond the heights. We cry aloud, and the only answer is the echo of our wailing cry. From the voiceless lips of the unreplying dead there comes no word; but in the night of death hope sees a star and listening love can hear the rustle of a wing. He who sleeps here, when dying, mistaking the approach of death for the return of health, whispered with his latest breath, 'I am better now.' Let us believe, in spite of doubts and dogmas and tears and fears that these dear words are true of all the countless dead." (Col. R. G. Ingersol's Great Speeches, pg. 67.)

There is no conflict between the Bible and true science. Theories of science may sometimes differ from the Bible. Science must theorize; and her theories of today are, many times, discarded tomorrow. We are learning all the time. If the time ever arrives when men of science have a perfect knowledge of the world, all apparent conflicts will disappear; and on the title page of every science textbook may be written:

"IN THE BEGINNING GOD."

Decision of the Audience

At the close of this, the last session of the debate, the chairman, F. L. Paisley, stated that a vote had been taken at the close of the first session, because of Mr. Smith's desire. Mr. Smith had later requested that no more votes be asked. "But now," said Mr. Paisley, "we are going to give the audience a chance to vote, by request of the Christian side of the discussion." The vote stood: Two for Smith; the rest of the audience for Oliphant.